The Winning Mindset for Leadership

Dennis Alimena, Ph. D.

iUniverse, Inc.
New York   Bloomington

The Winning Mindset for Leadership

Copyright © 2008 by Dennis Alimena, Ph.D.

All rights reserved. No part of this book may be used or reproduced by any means, graphic, electronic, or mechanical, including photocopying, recording, taping or by any information storage retrieval system without the written permission of the publisher except in the case of brief quotations embodied in critical articles and reviews.

The views expressed in this work are solely those of the author and do not necessarily reflect the views of the publisher, and the publisher hereby disclaims any responsibility for them.

iUniverse books may be ordered through booksellers or by contacting:

iUniverse
1663 Liberty Drive
Bloomington, IN 47403
www.iuniverse.com
1-800-Authors (1-800-288-4677)

Because of the dynamic nature of the Internet, any Web addresses or links contained in this book may have changed since publication and may no longer be valid. The views expressed in this work are solely those of the author and do not necessarily reflect the views of the publisher, and the publisher hereby disclaims any responsibility for them.

ISBN: 978-0-595-50629-3 (pbk)
ISBN: 978-0-595-49957-1 (cloth)
ISBN: 978-0-595-61589-6 (ebk)

Printed in the United States of America

Contents

Preface	ix
Introduction	1
PART ONE: ON AWARENESS	**3**
Yoda and Yogi	4
The Leadership Mindset	7
The Art of Perception	10
Learning to Get A-Head … Get It?	19
On HuManomics	23
On Mental Discipline	27
Know Thyself	29
Responsibility Psychology	31
Mind Pygmalion	33
The Next Level	36
Life Is But a Dream	40
PART TWO: ON CREATING THE WINNING MINDSET	**41**
Progress Toward Perfection	42
Love the Work	44
On Fatal Distractions	46
On Being Fearless	48
Playing to Win	50
On Human Nature and Motivation	54
The Boiled Frog Awareness	56
Mindset for Success	60
Get Good	62
Believe in Yourself	64
As a Person Thinketh	66
Who's in Charge?	69
The FUD Factor	71
On Focus	73
Be Here Now	75
Going Fast by Slowing Down	77
Slowing Down to the Speed of Effectiveness	82
PART THREE: ON TAKING ACTION	**85**
Observe	86
Preparation for the Winning Mindset	88

Trusting Yourself	90
Flow	91
Overthinking	93
Paradox and Performance	95
Performance Choice	99
The Inner Edge	101
The Hero's Journey	104
On Playing to Win	106
The Contest	108
Your MBS Degree and the Mirror Test	110
The Big Win in The Big Picture	113
The End of the Beginning	114
Bibliography	115
Footnotes	119

The Winning Mindset for Leadership: unlocking your potential in business, sports, and life

To Gary, sports psychologist and friend

To my family, Diane, Demi, Dana, and Tim

All are sources of inspiration…

Preface

My journey started when I took my first psychology class and got hooked on trying to understand myself and what motivated others. Sports and the classroom were great laboratories and a master's in counseling psychology helped me understand individual behavior even better.

Once anyone studies individuals, they will be led to groups, and that is where advanced studies in group dynamics took me. Sports and business highlight performance for individuals and groups of people. It has been and continues to be an exciting and diverse field of play and work.

I have been fortunate to work with some of the great companies of the Fortune 500 and many smaller enterprises as well. Work in Singapore, Kuala Lumpur, Geneva, Paris, London, Edinburgh and all throughout the United States has made me realize the great connection the human race has to one another. Lesson learned: there is far more that connects all of us than separates us.

Therefore, the lessons in this book are meant to be universal for any person in any organization, sports team, community, or family on this fragile planet. They are particularly powerful for anyone trying to lead … their life or any organization.

Introduction

WORK. WORK. WORK. That is the Puritan work ethic that has helped America and many other nations be productive. As a result, many good things have come to life for the hard working. It isn't a guarantee of success, but it doesn't hurt, and many would say that hard work helps build character. Even if you are lazy, you want people to think that you are hard working.

Inclusion. People generally like to be part of a group. There is safety in numbers, and human interaction is a craving that most rather enjoy … most of the time. People provide companionship, camaraderie, and a forum to sell to.

What if working in large groups and the inherent stress of that work was fatal? Would you search for an alternative? Look at page 38. There is a chart that should raise your eyebrows. What is happening to people in organizations that is shortening their lifespan? Or, are we in organizations shortening our own lifespan? What is the "winning mindset" when working in an organization (as many do)?

The Winning Mindset! Who doesn't want and need one? Yet, there are challenges and complexities—even paradoxes—that prevent a winning mindset. Each of us appears to have a success mechanism inside our psyche. If we follow that success mechanism that acts like a homing device, we lead an accomplished and successful life. Concurrently, a failure mechanism exists that can lead us down a frustrating and tormented path in our lives regardless of our talent. The Native Americans had a wise tale that mirrors this possibility:

An old Cherokee Indian teaching his grandson about life stated the following: "Within me there is a fight going on … It is a dreadful fight between two wolves. The one wolf is bad—made up of anger, jealousy, sorrow, regret, greed, self-satisfaction, resentment, ego …
The other wolf is good—he is joy, peace, humility, benevolence, truth, compassion, and faith … Within you the same fight rages—and the same applies to all people."

The grandson reflected on all this and asked, "Which one will win?"

The old Cherokee replied, "The one that you feed."

There are arrows that point us in the right direction, food for success or failure, in sports, business, and our home life. *The Winning Mindset for Leadership* is a collection of stories from the field of athletics, business, and home life that provide you with an opportunity to reflect on which wolf you are feeding. Also, there are questions labeled **So what?** for you to compare your own experience to, then make adjustments and make the most out of the potential that you have been given. In short, you can search for your own winning mindset in the process of reading this book.

This book is about taking a responsible look at work life and suggests that you are the key. How you think and behave is the solution to the lifespan challenge and all the experience that comes your way via business, family, community, and, in short, life.

After all, if you were to gain the world, but lost the most important relationships in the process, what would you have gained?

The book is divided into three parts. Part One is On Awareness. According to Eckhart Tolle and his new book, *A New Earth*, awareness and ego are incompatible.[1] Once you are aware of a better way of thinking, you will move beyond any unhealthy thinking that may be holding you back from winning. Part Two is On Creating a Winning Mindset. A winning mindset requires discipline and focus. If you get this far through the book, you have perseverance. Keep going. Part Three is On Taking Action. I once heard a very wise man say that in five years, you will be pretty much the person you are now, except for the people you meet and the books you read. Keep good company! And another wise piece of advice comes from the Far East: "To know and not to do is not yet to know." Take action and move toward your potential.

PART ONE: ON AWARENESS

Yoda and Yogi

WAS YODA RIGHT or was Yogi?
Yoda, of Star Wars fame, said there was no try, only do or do not. Yogi, of Berra fame, said that if you come to a fork in the road, take it.

The key to individual performance success may lie in these two very different pieces of advice. Your energy as measured by your behavior and your thoughts are the determinants of success, whether you are an athlete, business person, or family member. Yoda was talking about commitment. Commitment is a key trait that is measurable. When employee commitment was measured in one international fast food business, the food tasted better to customers. Let me repeat that: the more committed the employees were to the success of the business, the better the food tasted to customers. Commitment matters; there is no try.

Who knows what Yogi Berra[2] was really trying to say? But, many of us love his wit and complexity. Humor and paradox are two elements that we will explore later in this book. Perhaps Yogi was having fun while conveying an important message. During challenging times, humor and an appreciation for complexity will be needed. When you come to a fork in the road, you will need to decide ... take it.

Leadership occurs at every level and decision point in an organization, sports team, community, or family. Some may think you need direct reports to be a leader. You can see an example of this mindset at a Fortune 500 company that stated everyone was a leader. When the company constructed a sign at the crosswalk on its campus that read "Leader Crossing," nobody in the organization would cross at that crossing. People thought it was reserved for the leaders.

Everyone is a leader and everyone has a role. It is just that some leaders have larger responsibilities and influence than others. Organizations need to have a vision and strategic plan that focuses the energy of the organization. Otherwise, chaos ensues. As an individual, you need a strategy to focus your energy and align with the organizational purpose. For example, people in manufacturing need to put out the best product possible and meet the demands of customers; finance, information technology, human resources, operations, and all staff functions need to execute their part of the corporate dance. Sales and service are the interface with the client, the sine qua non of the business life cycle. Without customers, there is no business.

Individuals within each function have an individual role within their organizational function. That can often be forgotten.

The best test for an organization can be a merger. Two organizations trying to combine their energies is a great challenge. Four mergers that I witnessed were the HP and Compaq merger, the Bristol Myers and Squibb merger, the Glaxo and SmithKline merger, and the Bell Atlantic and NYNEX merger. All were clients, and it was fascinating to watch the interpersonal dynamics and leadership facilitate the complex process of merging.

Unlike a baseball or basketball game where the boundaries are outlined and the rules are clear, business has a thicker rule book and complexity, but effective leaders have the ability to see through the complexity and keep it simple. Carly Fiorina, the former CEO at HP, was constantly trying to find the simple elements of business that she could focus the organization on. Her background was Renaissance art and literature at Stanford, along with an MIT business degree, and she often said that her discipline learned in that field helped her see the simplicity she needed to focus on in business. Although controversial, she was a successful leader.

Simplicity should not be confused with a simplistic approach. The following quote from Oliver Wendell Holmes puts simplicity in the proper perspective and creates a proper aim for leaders: "I wouldn't give a fig for simplicity that lies on this side of complexity, but I would give my life to understand the simplicity that lies on the other side of complexity."

Got it? Hurry, let's move on to speed. There is such an emphasis on speed today that some organizations, individuals, and teams are rushing toward the future. They may not be sure what they are rushing toward, but they are in a hurry and will get there fast! Without wisdom, purpose, and effective leadership, these organizations, individuals, and teams may be rounding the bases to bankruptcy or organizational chaos.

The emphasis for this chapter is the mental aspect of the business mind. How do you know if you are rounding the bases to success, bankruptcy, breakdown, or breakthrough?

Yogi Berra said, "Ninety percent of the game is half mental." The challenge of the mental game is discovering what percent of what you do is mental. There is part of what you experience that you would say, like Walter Cronkite, "That's the way it is." You would not debate this "reality." You would simply accept it at face value. You believe it to be true.

Mark Twain had an interesting quip on this topic: "It ain't what you don't know that gets you into trouble. It's what you know for sure that just ain't so."

So most people would agree that much of what we do is mental and that the mental part can be the difference between success and failure. Look at the success of Tiger Woods, a professional golfer. You will have to admit that there is something special about his mindset that allows him to compete successfully against the best in the world.

Awareness is the key to achieving a winning mindset. Just by becoming more aware of what you are trying to achieve and your role in that success is a great starting point and a great changing point.

How to use this book

The following chapters are full of business, life, and sports anecdotes. Stories are helpful ways to connect with you because you have a story, too. Our stories connect us, so even though I am telling a story about a leader somewhere, or sharing a personal experience, you can relate, learn, and connect through your own experience and stories.

The questions posed in each section as "So what?" should be answered. Mark this book, dog-ear sections, and write down your insights. Francis Bacon said that the faintest ink is better than the best memory. This discipline will allow you to journal on your own mindset and make any adjustments that you feel are needed. The wonderful opportunity ahead is that you can design a winning mindset for yourself. With awareness and some helpful pointers, you can exercise your current mindset into the winning mindset that you need to be great.

I apologize in advance for repetition that will occur throughout the book. These ideas are layered and overlap is unavoidable. One of the great challenges for our society today is understanding that in self-improvement, you must engineer redundancy (repetition) into the process (your life). This builds confidence, but flows against the grain of a mindset that is set to eliminate redundancy.

The Leadership Mindset

BUSINESS LEADERS, SPORTS figures, and parents need a certain mindset in order to be successful. When they are "in the groove" or "in the zone," they know decisions are easier. There is less stress and more peace and serenity, ease and grace. This is not to say that their jobs or decisions are "easy." It is that they know what they need to do and they do it.

Like an athlete performing well, it appears effortless, but there was much training and preparation to get them to the decision point. In the book *Journey to Ixtlan*, Carlos Castaneda speaks of a "cubic centimeter of opportunity." He is referring to the wisdom of knowing when there is an opportunity in front of you. The corollary in business is similar, when the many forces of business life conspire to test the mettle of a leader. Sports present a similar opportunity at numerous points. This is when the leadership mindset and the training that has produced that mindset must come into play. That is why I like to see effective leadership training as a "portable feast." You can take it with you wherever you go. Training your mind for the mindset you need to have in order to be successful as a leader in your field will determine how far you go. This could be why so many, including the ancient Greeks, believe sports participation develops character.

Each part of a business needs a particular mindset in order to be successful, e.g., finance, operations, human resources, IT, marketing, and sales. The same can be true of a community or family. Everyone plays a role. The business acumen that accrues as a person grows in their business life is invaluable, with each discipline giving a different perspective on the same business. Truly effective leaders need a complete systemic understanding of how the organization works as a totality. This comes with experience and an ability to see the big picture at the organization. Particularly in Western culture, we are very good at breaking the whole into parts to better understand a part of the whole. The problem is that we can forget to put it all together again. Nothing works in a vacuum, especially in organizational life. When something happens in sales, it is felt throughout the organization. The same happens when there is a problem in finance. Good leaders and great sales people understand that the whole and how of what they do affects the whole body of business. This understanding is not only good for business, but it gives meaning and purpose to every effort from every individual in the organization.

So, the leadership mindset needs to understand complexity and how the parts add up to the whole. This is often called a systemic mindset.[3]

The other fundamental for leaders is understanding the existence of paradox. Truth often shrouds itself in paradox. The leader understands this … and takes action. Facts are great and should be used whenever and wherever they are available—and there are always more facts that could be gathered. To avoid paralysis by analysis, leaders must choose and move forward. To paraphrase the Spanish philosopher Ortega: "Business is fired at us at point-blank range and we must choose."

Let's demystify the leadership mindset with a simple thought experiment:

Bring to mind a time in business, sports, or another part of your life when you excelled. For example, you led a successful project, you corrected a part of your game, you mended an important relationship, or you made a difficult sale. Now, think about the feelings you had and how the work appeared to get done. See the sights and hear the sounds of that success. Recall the decisions and moves made for that success.

Now, bring to mind a time in life when things went terribly for you. Think about how you felt in that circumstance. See the sights and hear the sounds of that challenge. Recall the decisions and moves that created that challenging experience.

Here is your question: What percentage of the difference in those performances had to do with physical/technical skill (finance skill, operations skill, marketing skill, etc.)? What percentage was mental?

Athletes and business leaders alike usually respond the same way. What percentage did you note? **And how much time do you train your mind for that successful leadership mindset?**

This is a very unique challenge since each person may have their own idiosyncrasies about how they interpret success and challenge, how they learn, and how they define leadership. So, let's create some common ground and understanding on the meaning for leadership.

Key Point #1: Inner excellence is a process and it requires discipline. The lack of discipline disqualifies people from being effective leaders. There are countless stories of tremendous talent existing in an undisciplined body and mind. The result is almost always the same: a train wreck or Shakespearean tragedy.

Shakespeare was a genius at portraying the human condition and all the tragedy that could occur. The business environment, sports, and our communities play out some of that tragedy as well. Once when I was working with an executive in a Fortune 100 firm, after watching the drama unfold for his team, he reflected and said, "This is a Shakespearean tragedy unfolding." Fortunately, your life and your role in business can have a happier ending. The choice is yours.

So what?
- At peak performance, most of the game is mental. Discipline is needed to be effective. Is it in you? Are you disciplined?
- For your own journey and understanding, stop here and reflect on your own experience regarding discipline and mental preparation.
- Write down how you see the role of discipline in your success journey (where are you heading?).

The Art of Perception

NOTHING IS so fascinating (and frustrating) as the variability of human behavior and perception. Most are familiar with the Gestalts used to talk about human perception, with the most famous being the Old Lady/Young Lady:

In the gestalt on the left, people either see a "young lady" or an "old hag." What do you see? Now notice how the interpretation of the parts depends on how you interpret the whole. For example, if you interpret the sketch as a "young lady," how do you identify the part circled? If you interpret it as an "old hag," what is the part circled? The same data—or the same piece of "evidence"—is interpreted in different ways, depending on how you interpret the whole thing.[4]

There are other ways to explore the phenomenon of human perception. Here are a few examples:

- **Collage.** Put a bunch of pictures on a poster board or PowerPoint slide; show the collage to a group of people and ask what they see in a five-second exposure. People will be drawn to different colors, shapes, positioning, and words that may appear.
- **Fs exercise.** Choose a statement that has lots of Fs in it (especially the word "of"); ask people to count the Fs. No matter how long you let people count; some will not see all the Fs. How many Fs are in this bullet point? Hint: It's a magic number.

- **Magic Eye posters.** You stare at the picture until a three-dimensional image pops out at you. Some see the image easily, some never see it. Google "Magic Eye posters" for some cool tests of your ability.

Ever been in a conversation and someone took something totally different from it? Ever seen an accident and have eye witnesses see something different?

Woody Allen said that the greatest film ever made was *Roshomon* by Akira Kurosawa, telling the story of a witnessed killing and the conflicting testimony of witnesses. (Today, because of the movie, we talk about the Roshomon effect as the different recollections of the same event.) These stories and your own experience reflect the human challenge of effective communication. The mind and perception can be a tricky and frustrating thing. With awareness on your side, you can better understand what may be happening to you or your group and overcome this communication challenge.

A relatively easy model of how the mind and thought processes work was promoted by psychologists Roger Mills and George Pransky. Syd Banks was an originator of the model of Mind, Thought, and Consciousness, and Roger and George have been using the concepts in their practice for years with impressive results.

The metaphor that worked best for me from experiencing their work was the old 35mm film projector that used to be at the back of movie theatres. The mind is represented by the projector. The film represents thought that inevitably runs through the projector (like thoughts run through our minds). The light bulb represents consciousness because none of the thoughts come to life for us until our consciousness illuminates the little rascals.

Obviously, this school of thought does not believe in the Freudian approach. They focus on the here and now and where you want to go. Personally, it seems to work for most people. And most people that are in business need some level of healthy functioning to get to a position of responsibility and leadership. The projector metaphor has elegant simplicity and has helped people in business, sports, communities, and families better understand their own thinking and behavior.

On self-talk

Key Point #2: Pay attention to the messages that you are delivering to your mind. Your mind is emotionless and acts upon

the thoughts like they are real. That is why positive affirmations, reflection, timeouts, and prayer work. From years of study in human performance, this is now clear.

Eastern mystics have used mantras for centuries. The *man* in mantra is Sanskrit for mind. A mantra is a statement repeated over and over again (especially when you sense a negative thought is sneaking into your perfectly designed successful leadership mind). Mantras are useful anywhere, but particularly if you feel a lack of confidence or inferiority, and who doesn't at one time or another?

Self-talk is part of self-leadership. Although the term is not unique, the idea of leading oneself and being attentive to self-leadership dynamics is not as common. Self-leadership is connected to emotional intelligence. Much has been written on emotional intelligence (EI). Self-awareness and self-management is part of EI or what is also known as EQ (as compared with IQ). What is your EQ? And with a well-developed EQ, research indicates you will have an edge in being successful. Let's call this your Leadership Edge. The next section will help you explore this potential edge.

The leadership edge

What are the qualities that lead to an edge in today's busy world at home and in the business world? The edge that will be explored here is an invisible force. It comes from the inside out in a person. You cannot see these, but you can see the effect of the force. Like gravity, it is clear when it is at work. It is present in sports and business and examples will help highlight its effect. The seven forces of leadership have been present in most people's successful leadership journey. The forces are the mere shadow of the winning mindset. In sports, they have been referred to as the seven Cs.[5]

You can rate how well you are doing on a scale of one to ten, and you can consciously train your mind. It can be like having your own "indoor gym" program to build a better mindset, a winning mindset.

1. **Performance Force** (competitive mindset). This force comes from getting results and is part of an achievement energy or quest. This force understands the goals set forth and strives toward that end. The adaptation to this force is a competitive mindset. You have to enjoy competing to use this force constructively, and it's not necessarily about winning. There will always be someone better or, someone worse than you. The key is to love the competition. Bill Russell, the Hall of

Fame basketball center for the Boston Celtics, said that when he was in the heat of competition, it did not matter who won.[6] It could be this one fact that allowed Russell to win so many championships for Boston. On the business front, I remember Bristol Myers Squibb looking to double revenues and double sales by the year 2000. In 1996, many thought this was impossible without acquiring another organization. They did it and then got into a lot of trouble pushing the organization too far.

> Coaching tips for developing a **competitive mindset**: it is important to want to compete and push to make yourself better.
> -- Have a results orientation mindset, begin with the end in mind, have a vision/clarity of purpose.
> -- Focus and train your mind. Disciplined thought + disciplined action = envisioned result.
> -- Have an accountable mindset; ask yourself and your team, "What more can I/we do to get the performance result?"

2. **Relationship Force** (focused, control of emotions, emotionally intelligent). When individuals appreciate and influence the relationship force, mountains can be moved and great visions are realized. I once asked a successful real estate businessman what relationships had to do with being successful in business. His reply: "Everything." Human accomplishment involves many people. Even in individual sports, people behind the scenes make the accomplishment possible. Senior teams in business hold tremendous power, yet often the team is fragmented with various agendas. Sports teams can become fragmented as well in spite of having great individual talent. (Just observe some of the payrolls of major league baseball teams and their place in the standings.) When talent is combined with great relationships, it can be an easy and graceful ride to success.

Coaching tips for a **relationship mindset**:
- There is a logarithm for each person's relationship power. As you increase your relationship power, that logarithm increases. With that increase, your results will grow exponentially, not incrementally. How well are you connected?
-- One definition of successful leadership is to take people where they would not go on their own, yet in the end know they did it themselves.
-- Collaboration. Adopt FirstTeam[7] mindset across functions; play for the biggest win. Individual goals can get in the way of team goals. For example, the solution for the technology group may short circuit what the sales group is trying to accomplish. The two individual leaders need to collaborate like two teammates on a basketball team. Add seven teammates with big roles and big egos, and you can begin to appreciate the complexity and challenge in running large organizations well.

3. **Paradox Force** (courage). As mentioned earlier, leaders must understand that paradox exists. It is woven into the fabric of reality. A wise leader sees the paradox, understands the truth that lies on both sides, and decides a course of action. That may be what effective leadership boils down to in all cases. Proctor & Gamble is a very successful consumer business. Interestingly, they have products that compete with each other for shelf space in your local grocery stores. This may seem counterintuitive to some, but P&G has made it part of their culture. Long ago, the company leadership saw both sides of this conflict, yet they had the courage to chart a course of action that has been very successful for the company.

Coaching tips for a **paradox mindset**:
- Simplicity: seeing through complexity (paradox) to the simplicity on the other side.

- Courage: it takes courage to make a decision and move forward in an environment of uncertainty; be bold.

4. **Healthy Humor Force** (composure). On July 19, 1989, Captain Al Haynes was flying United 232, a DC-10, over Sioux City, Iowa. A crack in the rear engine blew and all hydraulics drained out. There was no way to steer the airplane. A DC-10 flight instructor happened to be on the airplane and the pilot, co-pilot, and flight instructor worked together to turn engines on and off to guide the plane. The strategy had never been tried. Upon approaching the airport, the control tower asked which runway Captain Haynes would use. His reply was, "Now you want me to choose a runway?"

    Coaching tips for a **healthy humor mindset:**
    - There is "above the line" humor and "below the line" humor.
    - Healthy humor is light and does not take advantage of any ethnic or religious group. It is inclusive and rated PG. Inclusive humor means that you include yourself (self-deprecating humor), or you help people laugh at themselves. Unhealthy humor isolates people and humiliates them in some way. You know it when you see it and experience it.
    - Take your job seriously and yourself lightly

5. **Change Force** (committed). Change happens everyday and we are all changing constantly. Hence the old saying that nothing stays the same or the Native American saying, "You never step into the same stream twice." Yet, paradoxically, human beings resist change even if the change is for the better. Albert Einstein and Thomas Edison resisted their own theories and inventions later in their lives as new physicists and inventors took their creations to the next level of understanding. Carly Fiorina revealed how difficult it is to change the order of things in the telecom business (AT&T and Lucent), and eventually in the computer business as CEO and Chairman of Hewlett-Packard. The bottom line

to effectively taking advantage of the change force is to be extremely committed to the change effort. Jack Welch transformed GE when he first took over as CEO in 1981. He believed that as the leader, he needed to exaggerate the change in order to get the organization to move effectively. For twenty years, he was a constant change advocate until his retirement in 2001. Tiger Woods changed his golf swing after winning the Masters. Great competitors have a change mindset and are constantly learning how to get better.

>   Coaching tips for a **change mindset**:
>   - Acknowledge and preach that nothing stays the same.
>   - The only thing that stays the same is change; look for examples, share them often, and use stories of successful change.
>   - Embrace change as your friend; become a Change Master, your God-given right as a natural-born leader.

6. **Customer-centric Force** (consistency). For business, the best example of customer service and the difference it can make is a little business on the Seattle waterfront called Pike's Fish Market. Fish is a commodity. Yet people will line up to buy fish at Pike's Fish Market because it is a different experience. The employees have fun there, and they let the customer in on that fun. The challenge is to consistently provide a great customer experience. This requires a disciplined mind and body. In sports, some great athletes forget they are in the entertainment business. Fights with customers (fans) and other inappropriate behavior are examples of athletes losing their perspective and neglecting the customer-centric force. As the old saying goes, if you do not take care of your customer, your competition will.

>   Coaching tips for **a customer-centric mindset**:
>   - With no customer, there is no business.
>   - Develop a line of sight to the customer: how does what you do connect with the end users?

7. **Presence Force** (confidence). You need a healthy balance of confidence and humility. When you are overconfident, you are cocky and you will lose your way. When you are unsure of yourself, you communicate that to everyone around you without saying a word. This is the most difficult force to manage because it is not about what you do, but who you are. It is not about human doing, but about human being. Presence understands without asking questions, sees silence as a friend, and welcomes uncertainty. One can spend a lifetime trying to understand presence without fully comprehending.[8]

    Coaching tips for a **presence mindset**:
    - Humility: balance confidence with an understanding that you don't have all the answers.
    - Listening: in a fast-paced world, this is becoming a lost art and much appreciated when done well.
    - Being real: it's OK for me to be wrong.
    - Caring: people won't care what you know until they know that you care ... sincerely.

Each of these forces is invisible, yet a powerful energy. Rate yourself using a scale of one to ten (one being very low use of this energy and ten being a high use of energy). With practice and awareness, you can get stronger in any area. Strength in that area will serve you well in business, sports, and at home.

Think of this book as your mind gym, a place to work out and condition your thinking the way it needs to function to be successful in your workplace. You will find that the exercise will benefit your life. (It will be a portable feast). This will help you acquire skill and discipline over your own thinking.

Every mindset has a time and place where it will serve you well. Understanding the timing and application of your mindset comes with experience. This wisdom cannot be taught, but must be "caught." And how do you get there? How do you get to Carnegie Hall? Practice. Practice. Practice. And business and life gives you plenty of opportunity to practice. The question is, "Are you mindful of what you are doing or are you on autopilot?" Albert Einstein said that if you continue to do what you are doing, you will continue to get what you are getting. As many have heard, one definition of insanity is continuing to do the same thing over and over and expecting different results. In Part One, you are becoming aware of the current mindset you are using to get results. If you are looking for a desired mindset to become even more effective, answering the questions and reflecting on the coaching tips, leadership forces, and key points will make a difference. As Gary Mack, a sports psychologist, said: **Learn to use your mind or your mind will use you.**

So what?
- How did you score yourself overall on the seven forces? Use the following scores as a guide:

63–70	Excellent
56–62	Good
49–55	Average
Below 49	Below Average

- How did you score individually? Any score at six or below indicates a need for more awareness and discipline around that energy.
- Are you aware of your awareness?

Learning to Get A-Head ... Get It?

UNDERSTANDING WHAT IT takes to be successful in business is something that everyone has an opinion on. The stories are similar, and please continue to ask people what it takes to be successful in your business. The themes will start to look the same. You will find areas that you believe you do well in and areas that are a challenge. Keep asking and reflecting on your own style of getting things done. This is an exercise in decoding the success DNA at your organization. It is an exercise in understanding the culture and how things are done. It is not formalized in any way, but usually it is the unwritten rules that you must figure out. My colleagues and I have done that for organizations and the process is not difficult. There are some basic beliefs that can help guide your process. If you understand these basic belief fundamentals, which are all debatable, then you will do fine:

- Belief Fundamental #1. The nature of man (and woman) is to be great. All people want to make a difference and feel their life has meaning.
- Belief Fundamental #2. Successful leadership requires a mindset that involves the seven forces mentioned above.
- Belief Fundamental #3. There are only so many stories to tell, and we insist on telling them over and over again.

This last one may sound arrogant (I thought it was the first time I heard it), but those in the movie business know it is true. There are an infinite number of ways to tell the same story, so the powerful play will go on, and you will get to contribute a verse. The question is, "What will you contribute?"

Listen for the themes of the stories of success and failure in your organization. It will provide a blueprint of what to do and what not to do.

Getting ahead: vision and patience

Mental rehearsal has shown to improve performance virtually every time. Yet how many people have the discipline to mentally rehearse for business performance? I had the fortunate opportunity to work with a CFO of a Fortune 100 corporation who was a gifted leader but had a severe learning disability. He would start each morning doing mental exercises to prepare for the day. He overcame his disability by properly knowing his learning challenge, then focusing to get his mind and thoughts aligned with the thinking needed to get through his day successfully as the CFO.

This is the discipline that a team and organization may need if the organization suffers from its own form of Attention Deficit Disorder (ADD) or Attention Deficit Hyperactivity Disorder (ADHD). If this seems too far fetched, bring to mind any organization that you know of that can't seem to focus on what is on its collective plate, but grasps the nearest fad or flashy program that comes along only to discard that after an organizational change or shift in leadership. Effective leadership requires patience and vision. Any organization that moves quickly from one fad to another is missing one or both of these key elements.

Some of you may be saying, "But what about speed?" Business has increased the speed of execution and time to market. Speed is essential. As one book title proclaimed, "It's Not the Big That Eat the Small… It's the Fast that Eat the Slow."[9] There is even a magazine that caters to the fast culture (see *Fast Company*). Speed is important. One organization that I was working with had heard the saying from another consulting company, "Leave skid marks."

I simply asked one question: "If you are leaving skid marks, shouldn't you be sure that you are going in the right direction?" I had a coach in college that used to say this about the fastest kid on the team one year: "He can run out of position faster than anyone."

Let me relate another experience that demonstrates this point. I had a grandfather who lived in Daytona Beach, and I can remember visiting him one summer and going to a carnival where they had a fourteen-car racetrack set up in a figure eight. Each person paid money to get a controller for a car. The controller had a steering wheel that reacted to the track and your steering. If the car came to a curve and I did not turn my wheel, my car would stop. After so many laps, there was a winner. Here is what I discovered: If I focused on my car and did not worry about the other cars and how they were doing, I could go fast (and often win). If I became worried and looked at the other cars (if I got distracted), my car went slow. Since that experience many years ago, I often wonder how much time is wasted looking at what others are doing or, worse yet, becoming distracted by something that would take my focus off of "my car," my purpose, my vision, my discipline for reaching goals and objectives.

The paradox principle

I know there is a need in business to know what the competitors are up to. It is important to play for a "big win" beyond my responsibility in the organization (especially at the senior leadership level). This is the paradox of leadership in today's complex business world. It is very similar to the athlete who gets paid handsomely for reaching individual milestones, but who is also part of a team. Finding the right balance between individual contribution and team accomplishment is the "cubic centimeter of opportunity"[10] for all business leaders and teams. The successful athlete understands this as well as the successful business person. It is individual contribution plus team chemistry that equals high performance.

Back to visualization: In a fascinating study, basketball players were separated into three groups and asked to improve their foul shooting. One group practiced foul shots for sixty minutes, another group visualized shooting foul shots for sixty minutes, and the third group visualized thirty minutes and shot for thirty minutes.[11] As you might guess, the third group had the best improvement. But how many basketball coaches teach visualization or use it in performance improvement as much as they do the physical practice? Some do. Many do not.

How many business people use visualization to prepare for an important presentation, sales opportunity, or boss conversation? From my experience, too few, although Western business leaders are bringing in more and more Indian gurus to teach business leaders,[12] so perhaps a shift in awareness is coming.

The leadership edge

I had the opportunity to work with a Fortune 500 company on creating a program that would help two companies overcome their merger silos. In a year when these companies were losing five billion dollars of business due to patent expirations, this program survived the budget cuts. The employee survey from the 2,000 leaders was too supportive of the program for it to be cut.

What was the magic?

There was no magic. The program gave the participants, who happened to run 10–15 percent of the organization at each session, an opportunity to reflect, see the big picture at the organization, connect with a senior leader, and build relationships with colleagues from around the globe (each session was designed to be a microcosm of the organization).

This three-day process gave each participant an edge. We called it the leadership edge and since then I have seen countless references to it. Everyone wants the leadership edge. The leadership edge is the focus, vision, and discipline that we have discussed along with the seven forces of leadership. It's the *portable feast* of leadership training referenced earlier.

Mental skills need constant practice for the individual, team, or organization. Start with yourself, then invite your team, and someday the organization may want to start a new discipline in the 360 process: visualization.

So what?
- Are you moving fast?
- Are you moving in the right direction?
- Do you have a clear vision?
- Do you have the patience to avoid distractions and focus on the game?

Recommended activity to help shape a winning mindset:
- Read biographies of successful people. See the patterns of beliefs and behaviors that made them successful, and challenge yourself to bring those beliefs into your own life.
- At least once a year, set time aside for some self-improvement experience.
- Reflect and/or meditate.
- Practice yoga; try something new.
- Become disciplined in learning from your experiences.

On HuManomics[13]

"It is not where we stand in times of comfort and convenience that measures who we are, but where we stand in times of conflict and controversy."

—Martin Luther King

MANY OF YOU may remember Scott Hamilton. He is an Olympic Gold Medalist in figure skating. Scott was born a sickly child burdened with a rare digestive disease. During his Olympic gold medal performance, at 5'3" and 115 pounds, there he stood at the center of the rink. When asked what he was thinking at that time, Scott said it was time to go out and have fun. The hard work had been done. His mental preparation and discipline told him to relax and enjoy the moment and all that he had prepared for.[14] How many of you, when the pressure is on to meet a deadline, can feel yourself tense up? How many feel pressure to make money and pay the bills?

These responses make sense, but they can lead you down an unhealthy path if you are unaware. Pressure can lead to breakthrough or breakdown. Your thoughts will direct the result.

Dr. Hans Selye is considered the grandfather of stress research. He identified the stress response known as the General Adaptation Syndrome (GAS). This included adrenocortical enlargement (increase in adrenaline), atrophy of the thymicolymphatic organs (decrease in the immune system), and an increase in gastrointestinal acid.[15] The interesting aspect about stress is that you can think about stressful events and induce the GAS response. On the other hand, you can learn to relax and stay calm during a stressful event.

Stress does not have to be negative. Pressure can help you focus. It is one of the attractions of deadlines. If we did not have deadlines, we would have to create them because they motivate us to get things done. The problem is that we create deadlines and we have a tendency to forget that we created them, quite arbitrarily. How much stress in life and business is self-induced? And when you add the stress created by leadership that believes you need a "burning platform" to motivate people, you quickly see how much stress is of our own doing.

In medicine, it is known as an iatrogenic effect when an illness is physician- induced. Here is a frightening excerpt from a physician:

In 2000, there was a JAMA article (this is the American Medical Association's main journal), which estimated that 225,000 deaths occur every year in hospitals from unnecessary causes. Read that again ... almost a quarter of a million people dying at the hands of error. This is more than the number of people dying from lung cancer every year ... more than the number of people dying from stroke every year.

When it comes to health care ... What do I do?

1. I encourage everyone to question his or her medical care. If you feel like it's not right ... I guarantee it's NOT! Speak up.
2. I look up questions online and in the published literature searches, such as Pub Med. Many of the abstracts make sense and can easily be applied to your case.
3. I demand that everyone on the health care team use common sense and stick to the facts. If they don't know, they should say so and find out. [16]

People die each year in the hospital for reasons unrelated to their diagnosis or illness. This unintended consequence is a serious side effect of trying to do good. Leaders need to be aware of the unintended consequences of their decisions. Deciding to create a "burning platform" may lead to many unintended consequences (like burnout and low morale). I will concede that this strategy works in the short term and for some people, but it is just short sighted and not sustainable. The above suggestions for health care apply equally for your business strategy or project:

1. Question the thinking behind the strategy; if it is not clear, speak up!
2. Look up questions online; the Internet is a great place to explore.
3. Practice common sense, a beautiful thing that can often get lost in the emotion of business. As stated before, common sense does not mean common practice in organizational life.

Back to real pressure

A "closer" in baseball is the pitcher who comes in late in the game to preserve a lead. He comes into a pressure situation. Some business leaders are good at coming into a project or business and fixing it. Some people seem to thrive on the sense of urgency and chaos that dysfunction and some business situations may present. What may occur in some situations is that those who thrive in a pressure cooker may unknowingly create that experience for everyone when it may not be that "urgent."

It is not a question of *if*; it is a question of *when* there will be a breakdown.

If we have leaders creating burning platforms, isn't it any wonder that the workplace is stressful and de-energizing (and perhaps life shortening, see page 38). No human being thrives under pressure all of the time. It is like jumping on a treadmill and running at full speed. Human beings simply cannot function that way.

Paradoxical principle

The probability that you will achieve an outcome increases when you let go of the need to have it. This principle flies in the face of our linear logical mind and what we have been conditioned to plan and prepare for. However, Gary Mack spent much of his time getting players who were not performing to relax and be less attached to the outcome. This allowed their natural talents to emerge and be realized. Many have performance anxiety and simply try too hard. Many business people are in this category as well.

Everything gets filtered. All experience must run through your own brain, be processed, and emerge in some form. Ilya Prigogine, a Belgian chemist, won a Nobel Prize for his theory of dissipative structures.[17] A manufacturing town is a dissipative structure in that materials are moved into the town, they are processed, and something is made or created and moved out of the town. Your brain is a dissipative structure. You take information in, process it, and do something with it. This happens unconsciously most of the time. What mental rehearsal can do is give you better control over the thoughts and images that come into your mind. One neurologist trying to help his patients with anger and depression called it controlling the ANT population in your mind. ANT stood for Automatic Negative Thoughts.[18]

Mental rehearsal, meditation, relaxation, prayer, or whatever methodology you use to slow down and reflect can give you better control over your thoughts, which will affect your attitude, behavior, and mood.

So what?

- Where do you stand during times of conflict and controversy?
- What iatrogenic effect are you having on the organization and the people you are leading?
- What effect are you having on yourself? Are you healthy?
- Are you too attached to the outcome? What is creating the attachment?

On Mental Discipline

IN BUSINESS, AND certainly more so in sales, mental toughness is an important survival trait that allows a person to continue doing what is needed to be successful without taking the rejection personally. In the book *The Four Agreements*, Don Miguel Ruiz gives advice to people that was passed down from the ancient Toltec wisdom and tradition in his family. **These were agreements that you made with yourself** if you wanted to be successful in life. Here they are:

1. Be impeccable with your word, speak with integrity, have your words move toward truth.
2. Don't take anything personally; people project what is going on in their lives to you, so see the innocence, even in rejection of your product or business.
3. Don't make assumptions, ask questions, and summarize what you thought you heard.
4. Always do your best (and understand that your best may vary depending on your health, situation, and other outside factors).[19]

For healthy high performance in business as well as sports, mental toughness is an important trait. Mia Hamm, the great soccer player, said that the most important attribute a player can have is mental toughness. Chris Evert added, "Competitive toughness is an acquired skill and not an inherited gift."[20]

Most would agree that mental toughness is important for success, especially as your work becomes subject to more scrutiny (as you climb the corporate ladder or ascend the pop charts with your latest hit). The challenge is to understand the difference between mental toughness and just plain being mean and/or cold hearted. In a recent business publication, CEOs that were hired to turn companies around were characterized by "toughness" and business people do not have to go back very far in their memory to recall what some of the "heroes" of the '90s did to some perfectly good organizations. Barbarians at the Gate, Rambo in Pinstripes, Only the Paranoid Survive were all products of this era. This is not the toughness that I am referring to here. If you review Jim Collins work, *Good to Great,* you can see a balanced look at what effective leadership should look like. Collins says that a unique combination of strong will (which we see plenty of in sales and business leadership) and humility (which is in short supply in corporate life in my opinion and experience) lead to sustainable results that dwarfed competitors in the same business over the same timeframe.[21]

Combining mental toughness with a good dose of humility appears to be the right combination. This is a paradox: the truth lies on both ends of this continuum, strong will and humility. Knowing when to invoke your will or humility comes with experience and good judgment, often known as wisdom. To clarify, wisdom has nothing to do with age or how long someone has been in a position. For a good review of intuitive knowing, see Malcolm Gladwell's *Blink*.

So what?
- Train your mind to continuously learn; be curious about what is around you versus judgmental.
- Reflect daily on what you have learned.
- Trust your intuition (your gut); for it is more intelligent than your brain will ever be.
- See your thoughts as friends that you can invite in or not; take yourself lightly and your job seriously.

Know Thyself

"If I had my life to do over again, I would not have as high a high or as low a low, but stay more in the middle."
—Leo Buscaglia, former USC professor

When I heard Leo Buscaglia say this on a PBS series, I was befuddled. Why would someone want to lessen their highs? As time has gone by, I am beginning to understand what Leo was saying. Phil Jackson, the Zen-like coach of the LA Lakers, says that he takes his pulse during a game and if it is getting too high, he calms himself down. He understands that his thinking is better in a calm state than in a frenetic state. Gary Mack understood this and stated that athletes perform on an inverted "U" known as the performance curve. If you were to graph performance, the vertical line would be numbered one to ten and represent performance and productivity; the horizontal line would be numbered one to ten and represent stress and arousal. Athletes understand that you cannot be too aroused or stressed or performance will be inhibited. Business leaders and sales leaders need to understand this delicate balance as well. But, most importantly, you need to understand it for you. This is self-leadership. Know your limits. Know when you need to calm down (like Phil Jackson) for clearer thinking and better performance.

Leo was vibrant and loved life. He would not trade the feeling for life as he experienced it for anything. He was looking for a higher overall quality that simply vibrated at a higher level. You need to learn to vibrate at a higher level. Watch the performers in your organization. Watch yourself. At what frequency do you want to be? Know your numbers.

In auto racing, there is a concept known as "redlining." This is when the engine is running at a high speed (rpms). Running an engine to the redline can be healthy (that is where maximum power exists), but to go beyond that redline for a long period of time is flirting with disaster. In business, we are pushing people and systems with the same risk. Effective leaders know when they have pushed too far. Effective self-leadership is about pushing yourself beyond your own comfort level, but not pushing yourself to the point of breakdown. Know your numbers.

Human beings respond to stress in a variety of ways. Gary Mack stated that there are cardiac responders (heart rate goes up), skin responders (skin begins to perspire), and kinesthetic responders (stomach churns, neck and back muscles tense)[22]. These are all early warning signs. Then, a little voice starts to feed your mind negative thoughts (an ANT attack)…

So what?
- Learn to recognize the early warning signs for you.
- Create something to replace the automatic negative thought (ANT), such as a positive mantra, that will be stating what you will do or who you are.
- Breathe deeply and connect with calm and peace (see a place that relaxes you).

Responsibility Psychology

RESPONSIBILITY PSYCHOLOGY HAS been called accountability in the business and sales world. It is one of the most powerful virtues that a person can possess. In a nation that easily points the finger at someone or something else, some have become victims to the action of others (in their own view). Accountability, or what is called responsibility psychology in this chapter, is an **individual personal mindset**. It is an "inside out" virtue that cannot be forced upon you. I like to think of this as a mindset because you have control over having it or not. It is a choice.

The best way to teach accountability is to be accountable. Since many of us learn by imitation, it is truly the best form of flattery when you see a team acting accountably and when asked why, they state, "Our leader wouldn't have it any other way."

There are many great resources on the topic of personal accountability. I see it as a personal virtue that should tie into the performance values of an organization. The question to bring more accountability into your life is: "What more can I do to get the result?" If you are leading a team or having a coaching conversation, the question becomes: "What more can we do to get the result?" If a leader can get all of his team members asking this question of themselves, the leader gets group accountability.

Beware of the Accountability Club! This sounds like an association (which could be a very good support group), but the warning here is not to use accountability to club somebody over the head.

- It is an inside out virtue.
- You can not force somebody to be accountable.
- "Holding someone accountable" is only a sentiment often used in business—well intentioned, but technically impossible to do

As the great Katharine Hepburn once stated, "You learn in life that the only person you can correct and change in life is yourself."

One of the greatest sayings ever was on the refrigerator of my grandmother and attributed to Reinhold Niebuhr (1892–1971), the philosopher and theologian: "God grant me the serenity to accept the things I cannot change, the courage to change the things I can, and the wisdom to know the difference." Richard Miller later amended this wise saying in his book on personal accountability to read, "God grant me the serenity to accept the people I cannot change, the courage to change the person I can, and the wisdom to know it is me."[23] This version places accountability where it should be: deep within the individual.

Mind Pygmalion

"The ability to conquer oneself is no doubt the most precious of all things sports bestows on us."

—Olga Korbut, Olympic gymnast

In sports psychology, there is a concept known as the sports consistency theory. It states that we act consistent to our self-concept—our self-image.[24] This is why it is important to listen to your self-talk and amend that talk to better shape your performance.

I remember watching Olympic gymnast Mary Lou Retton who stood preparing for her last vault on the pommel horse. She needed a perfect ten to capture the gold medal. Later, she was asked what she was thinking as she approached her final vault. Her response was a testament to her mental training and belief in herself: "Need a ten, got a ten."

Truly our worst enemy is often our own thinking. Zig Ziglar called it Stinkin' Thinkin' and encouraged his readers to give themselves a "check up from the neck up"— good advice for any business person regardless of position in the organization. Gary Mack called self-defeating thoughts "gremlins" and compiled a list from his experience. See if you recognize any of these. These are also known as the ANTs (automatic negative thoughts) mentioned earlier.

- **Fear.** Most have heard of the fight-or-flight response in human beings. It appears to be deeply embedded in our genetic make-up. There is a third possibility that you may have experienced or witnessed: freeze. The choice to do nothing is a choice and sends a message in business culture. When an underperforming employee is never dealt with, it sends a message loud and clear to the rest of the organization and gives the unintended permission for others to underperform. Most of the time, it is fear that prevents the leader from taking the necessary action. One of my favorite expressions in business is that common sense is not often common practice. Dealing with underperformance is common sense, but not common practice in many organizations.

- **Anger.** I coach executives about emotional level and intellectual level. Executives often value their intellect, so when I warn them, "The higher the emotional level, the lower the intellectual level," they get it. This barometer connects to Emotional Intelligence (EQ) that many corporations are turning to for part of their leadership development. Anger, frustration, and impatience are three gremlins that can get in the way of healthy high performance. Control your anger or it will control you.
- **Anxiety.** Guilt from the past and worry about the future is a sure-fire formula for anxiety, a waste of energy. Sure, you need to plan for the future, set aggressive goals, and learn from past experience. But some people seem to be wired for worry. You can train your mind to be worry-free. First, you must recognize the challenge, and then go about changing that mindset. You will find a new and exciting world beyond a worry mindset.
- **Self-consciousness.** Athletes have to take themselves lightly. Business people need to do the same. If you are concerned about "not looking good," you may play a game called *"Not to lose."* Football fans know what happens when their team is playing a prevent defense—it usually leads to a score for the other team. In my leadership work, I ask leaders to be vulnerable and let people see the human side of them. This, ironically, leads to people wanting to follow a leader once they see that they are human, fallible, just like them. This is counterintuitive (like leaning into a boxer's right hook).
- **Perfectionism.** This is a state not attainable by human beings. I encourage leaders to settle for excellence in themselves as well as others. I have never met a human being who thought they were perfect. Others may have thought that someone saw themselves as perfect, but something in the human genetic code (or common sense) does not allow us to see ourselves that way. Deep inside, we know we are fallible. Be real, authentic, and excellent.
- **Stubbornness.** This can result in an unwillingness to learn; there is a point when persistence turns into just plain stubbornness, like a bull. In finance, there is a time to cut your losses—don't throw good money after bad money—and this lesson works in sports and other parts of business well.
- **Lack of motivation.** This is where discipline comes in.

Billy Wilder, a successful director and Hollywood producer, said that he and his partner would come to the office every day and work from nine to five. Sometimes, they did not accomplish much, but on other days, characters were created and films developed. It was the discipline of working everyday that he attributed his film success. You have to do what you need to do even when you don't feel like it.

- **Competitiveness.** Talent will get you only so far, and then there must be a Factor X, some competitive fire that makes you go beyond what you thought you were capable of doing. When you are in the competitive flow, everything comes to a halt and even the score may disappear. Passion is often used when talking of someone's competitiveness.
- **Distractions.** Here is a discipline issue again. Life, business, and sports present us all with an infinite number of distractions. Can you focus on your preparation and execution?
- **Optimism.** Optimism has emerged as a key ingredient of effective leadership. This works for team leadership as well as self-leadership. This optimism is balanced with a realism and honesty of where you are currently. Remember, luck is when preparation meets opportunity.

So what?
- Put a checkmark beside the gremlins that are visiting your mind.
- Replace them with a positive affirmation.
- Move confidently forward to do what you know you can do.

The Next Level

MUCH HAS BEEN made recently about focusing on your strengths and mastering what you do well.[25] Although well intended, I have seen some business people use this as an excuse not to do something that they can get better at (and perhaps they simply don't like doing). If you look at the world of sports, you find examples of practice that made somebody better in an area of weakness, which then made the difference between being mediocre and excellent. Success in business involves a constant discipline of doing what others will not do or don't want to do. Cold calling and accepting rejection as part of the success formula is widely known and accepted by the successful sales people.

Earl Weaver was the great manager of the Baltimore Orioles and one of the most knowledgeable managers baseball has ever seen. He stated, "It is what you learn after you know it all that counts." And Knute Rockne, the great Notre Dame football coach, encouraged people by stating, "Build your weaknesses until they become your strengths."[26]

Some functions you may never master. This is known in the testing world as aptitude; you look at what you do well and match that aptitude against professions that require that skill. Richard Bolles has been revising his job search reference for years after he sought a career change after being displaced from his position in the church he was serving.[27]

Achievement is the second cornerstone of awareness. What have you done that was successful? What have been your "highs" thus far in your working career? This will give you some feedback on what you enjoy. Taking what you do to mastery level is a very good development plan. But that is only part of a good development plan. There is a story in the Far East that demonstrates this point:

> *Once there was a student who went to a great teacher to learn. The teacher offered the student a cup of tea. The student accepted and as the student was demonstrating their knowledge to the Zen master, the teacher kept pouring the tea into the cup while the water flowed over the cup into the saucer and onto the table. The student was puzzled.*
>
> *"Why are you still pouring the water, Master?"*

And the Master responded, "Your mind is so full of what you think you know that there is no room for new learning. You must learn to empty your mind of what you think you know if you ever hope to learn anything new."

Earl Weaver's comment is a Western way of saying the same thing. You must have the humility to let go of what you know in order to accept and let in new learning. This is not easy. Look at the resistance to new knowledge:

- The cure for scurvy was discovered 150 years before it became common practice in the British Navy to take fresh fruit on long voyages.[28]
- The practice of washing hands for physicians was resisted in spite of the data to support the practice.
- Drinking and driving or smoking tobacco are obviously bad ideas, yet look at the abuse and the lives negatively impacted by these bad habits (in sports as well as business)

The great paradox in life is that everything changes, yet we human beings are comfortable with the way things are and defend keeping things the same even at the risk of life and limb. Machiavelli warned of this tendency years ago when he gave this ominous advice to a potential leader. The advice is good even today if you are attempting something new:

> "It must be considered that there is nothing more difficult to carry out, nor more doubtful in success, nor more dangerous to handle, than to initiate a new order of things. For the reformer has enemies in all those who profit by the old order, and only hesitating defenders in all those who would profit by the new order, this hesitation arising in part from the fear for their adversaries, who have laws in their favor; and partly from the incredulity of mankind, not truly believing in anything new until having actually experienced it."[29]

Your competition will always find your weakness and exploit it. If you are managing a product, be aware of its strengths and weaknesses. When evaluating yourself, be objective, ask for feedback, encourage open and honest dialogue. There is too much bull in today's work environment and political atmosphere. People are trying not to upset the apple cart, being polite, and not speaking the truth to one another. This can lead to a passive-aggressive culture where everyone politely nods in agreement, but never really backs an idea.

Somebody has to stop this culture of polite compliance. It has been going on for so long in some cases that people cannot even see it. This is what I like to call an "unhealthy normal" state in the organization.

Some jobs are absolutely insane (meaning highly impractical and unhealthy). Yet, people continue to work at such jobs, rationalizing that if they don't do it, the company will hire someone else. This may be true; however, most companies would like to think they value their people and most leaders would not like to think they are purposely shortening the lifespan of their longtime employees. Look at the data from several large firms on life span and retirement. If you just arrived from Mars and looked at this data, what would it suggest?

Age of Retirement	Average Age of Death
49.9	86
51.2	85.3
52.5	84.6
53.8	83.9
55.1	83.2
55.1	82.5
56.4	81.4
57.2	80
58.3	78.5
59.2	76.8
60.1	74.5
61	71.8
62.1	69.3
63.1	67.9
64.1	66.8
65.2	

The chart indicates that for people retired at the age of fifty, their average lifespan is eighty-six, whereas for people retired at the age of sixty-five, their average life span is only sixty-six. An important conclusion from this study is that for every year one works beyond age fifty-five, one loses two years of lifespan on average.[30]

The Boeing experience is that employees retiring at age of sixty-five receive pension checks for only eighteen months, on average, prior to death. Similarly, the Lockheed experience is that employees retiring at age of sixty-five receive pension checks for only seventeen months, on average, prior to death. Dr. David T. Chai indicated that the Bell Labs experience is similar to those of Boeing and Lockheed based on the casual observation from the newsletters of Bell Lab retirees. A retiree from Ford Motor told Dr. Paul Tien-Lin Ho that the experience from Ford Motor is also similar to those in Boeing and Lockheed.[31]

Maybe that is why young people today are changing careers faster than you can say "Generation X" or "Millennial." Maybe it is a survival instinct that is kicking in that keeps the average employee on the move today. It is estimated that a business school student today can anticipate fourteen career changes in their lifetime. That is a far cry from previous generations who went to work for one company. To change companies was a big deal. Today it is like changing your underwear.

These are organizational challenges because there is a war going on for talent at the same time that young business people are looking for a new deal from their employers—challenging assignments, growth opportunities. The bottom line is that organizations are trying to respond, but the matter rests with each individual. Development is personal. Be accountable and develop yourself.

In Japan, the term "kaizen" means continual improvement. This means looking at your whole skill set and taking on the challenges that will make you a better business person.

So what?
- Ask yourself what improvement you need in your mindset to help get you where you want to go.
- Go on; get out of your comfort zone.

Life Is But a Dream

VISION IS CRITICAL for business leaders and the organizations they serve, but it is critical for you, the individual, as well. Regardless of your place in the organization, you need goals and dreams to pull you into the future. This idea of "future pull" is philosophically opposite from the "burning platform." The burning platform was an idea discovered when people would willingly dive into the frigid waters of the North Sea from an oil rig that was on fire. Many leaders believe that people will change only when there is a "burning platform."

John Kotter from Harvard University recently wrote the book *Our Iceberg Is Melting*. It's a different metaphor but the same idea of creating action around a crisis, a crisis that may be real. This is not meant to criticize, but to address the key to connecting with a potential motivational button.

Future Pull is the idea that there is a future so exciting that you cannot wait to get there. The energy and concurrent motivation created by Future Pull is very different than the Burning Platform. I believe people long for that positive force. If your organization is not providing that positive energy, then it is up to you to create it for yourself.

Gary Mack, sports psychologist, had an acronym that he liked to use: ACT.
- **A**ccept your present state; accept your strengths and weaknesses.
- **C**reate your desired state; what is your dream?
- **T**ake action; success is a journey and enjoy the ride.

Johnny Bench, Michael Jordon, Spike Lee, and Martin Luther King all created their own vision and dream of what they wanted. Marcia Weider, a success coach, wrote a book called *Life Is But a Dream*. She talks about dream teams, being a dreamer, and dream magic. There is great value in visioning and dreaming.

So what?
- What are your goals?
- What vision do you have for your position? Your company? Your career? Your family?
- What is your vision for the dream in you?
- Can you ACT?

PART TWO: ON CREATING THE WINNING MINDSET

Progress Toward Perfection

Perfection. What a lofty vision! In baseball, a perfect game is when the pitcher gets all twenty-seven outs in a game with no hits or walks or errors—nobody reaches base. That is perfection and is known as a "perfect game." What is your perfect game?

Now if there is a couch nearby, go relax because this may take some time to figure out (paradox always does). A perfect game, by baseball standards, does not mean that everything was perfect. There were balls thrown that were not strikes. There was wasted movement by other players, signs missed, and a vendor ran out of popcorn. But the essence of perfection remained, and the bottom line was "perfect."

How would you define perfection for you? At a consulting company I worked at for twelve years, we encouraged leaders to replace perfection with excellence. It was more realistic in our minds. However, some leaders like to use the word Perfection. When properly defined, it can have some motivating value and provide a vision. Alan Feldman, CEO at Midas International, used this quote many times over his executive career: "Be sure to recognize people and progress on the way to perfection." This was part of his leadership philosophy. He saw perfection as a quest.

Success studies reveal that goals are central to any successful endeavor—sports, business, or any dimension of life. However, goals need to be SMART. Here is a helpful acronym that you can use to properly set your own goals:

> **S – Specific.** Perhaps your vision is to run a division of the company, then you may want to be the best project manager on an important initiative, or sharpen your financial skills by attending a certification program in finance. In sales, your vision may be to become the best sales person in your region,
>
> **M – Measurable.** In sales, you may want to set a goal of X number of presentations next week, next month, this year. In sports, you might practice taking one-hundred ground balls every day. You set your mind to do the work that will lead to your desired result.

A – Achievable. The art of setting goals is that they are possible for you to reach, and they are under your control. The great quality guru, Edwards Deming, used a red bead experiment where he stated that manufacturing red beads was the goal. The red and white beads were mixed up in a box and the participant could not see which beads they were pulling from the box. His point for manufacturing was that you needed control over the quality; otherwise you could not expect the workers to hold themselves accountable. Your goals need to be under your control.

R – Realistic. This is simple. It needs to be believable. This belief needs to reside in you and not in the press or family or team. As the Gatorade commercial clearly asks, "Is it in you?"

T – Time-bound. When? Your goal must have a time boundary and timeline. Deadlines can be beautiful things. Use them to your advantage in place of seeing them as dragons to be slain.

As Gary clearly stated with his athletes and I am stating for you here:

Goals are dreams with a timeline.

So what?
- Are your goals SMART?
    - Specific
    - Measurable
    - Achievable
    - Realistic
    - Time-bound

Love the Work

On his deathbed, Sigmund Freud said that the most important things in life were love and work. With the amount of time that people devote to work, it only makes sense that you should truly love what you are doing. Yet many accept their fate to be at some job or existing at some company doing work that does not fulfill them, but only provides a paycheck. Now, I understand the paycheck is important, but to think that you have to do something that underutilizes your talent and potential is selling yourself drastically short.

One of the great ironies in the corporate world is that there is a war for talent going on and there is incredible potential within the very organization that is warring for talent. It is like the family that lived in poverty for generations while underneath their poor dilapidated home there was the richest deposit of wealth in the world. I can't help but think that same scenario (and tragedy) is unfolding within each large corporate organization and in each developing country as well. Genius is everywhere ... including inside of you!

Find your passion and what you are good at, and you will find your genius and a way to make a living while having a blast. My favorite definition of success is being able to do what you love ... and get paid for it. It may not be an easy journey. Martin Luther King spoke of the "furnace of adversity" that the Civil Rights movement went through in the '60s. Perhaps it is true that adversity forges character.

Adversity reveals a lot; prosperity hides a lot.

So, don't shy away from adversity or hard work. It may be the door you need to go through to achieve your vision.

Overnight success
Everyone wants to be successful. We are all envious of the overnight success of a business idea, sports personality, or model. I have come to believe that this is largely a myth. When you interview these successes, you usually find a long journey that preceded the success.

Lars Anders wrote in his paper, "Deliberate Practice," that it takes about ten years of practice to acquire the mastery of an expert.[32] Other performance experts point out that the "experts" practice about ten times more than the amateur. I have a friend who is a good golfer. I asked him how he hits so well out of the sand. He stated simply, "Well, I hit one-hundred balls out of the sand." When I practiced hitting balls out of the sand, I got much better as well. Most of us love a story about overnight success when in reality it is often the result of hard work and hard practice. Are you willing to pay the price for the success you desire?

You can have it all ... just not at the same time! You must choose.

It is estimated that we make anywhere from two to five thousand decisions a day. Most happen unconsciously or without much thought. We are on auto-pilot. Your future is too important. What decisions (choices) are you making that influence where you are today? Get off auto-pilot and get on course toward your vision and goals!

So what?
- If you have been disciplined to this point, you should have outlined your vision and your goals. Now it is time to think about the choices that you make.
- Be aware of each choice and the impact that choice has on your goals and vision. That awareness will lead you to better choices.
- Move in the direction of those better choices.

On Fatal Distractions

IF THESE SECTIONS were chapters, this would be chapter thirteen, and it should be called something negative, shouldn't it? Some buildings don't have a thirteenth floor and a distraction from your goals is a metaphorical thirteenth floor for your success. Distractions come in all shapes and forms. Some are subtle, and some are so obvious that it is embarrassing to have to mention them. But, once again, common sense does not translate to common practice.

Smoking and alcohol or drug abuse are the first two common-sense warning signs. It is still a great bewilderment to me why so many people choose to smoke and to overindulge in alcohol and drugs, and risk their health and success. As a counselor to kids in high school for three years in a small school outside Philadelphia, I witnessed a tragedy each year when an accident either paralyzed or killed a high school athlete. It always involved alcohol or drug abuse. The bottom line is always the same—poor judgment and catastrophic results. And we brought in all the experts to talk about the dangers of abuse, we had assemblies, we had the smashed car in front of the school, we had a MADD (Mothers Against Drunk Driving) organization, and the deaths continued. They continue today. Look at the headlines. There are premier athletes and successful business people constantly making the headlines with poor choices. Young actors and actresses seem to be particularly vulnerable to making poor choices, but I am sure there are examples in every discipline of sport and business.

Why? I have discussed this at length for athletes. Athletes, like some movie stars, have a way of coming to believe that they are above the law. I discussed my experience with adolescents and their belief that it could never happen to them. Accidents and catastrophes happened out there, but not here. They felt invulnerable. The same mindset was occurring at both levels. Athletes, students, and business people need to understand that everyone plays by the same rules. In legal language, it is called the Rule of Law and it is considered one of the basic rules for democracy to work.

Business has had its fair share of poor judgment over the past twenty-five years. When the truth comes out, we are all amazed at the arrogance of the mindset that created the crisis, e.g., Enron, World Com, Tyco, Global Crossing, and the list could go on and on. At this writing, the sports world is filled with performance enhancing drug accusations, and prominent athletes are having their records and medals taken away or their images badly tarnished. Time will tell whether these premier athletes tried to get an even better edge by making some poor choices.

The discipline to say NO!

When it comes to distractions, they can be very subtle. A phone call, a friend's visit, or a well-meaning family member can be the distraction that takes you off course. The blatant examples are the party invitation or the road trip or binge to escape what you need to do to be successful. Janet Evans is a gold-medal swimmer who admitted feeling envious of her friends going to parties when she would have to go to bed. Those sacrifices led her to three gold medals and an experience of a lifetime at the Olympics. Her comment: "It's definitely been worth it."

Kevin Johnson, a basketball star, went to the gym every evening to practice. One Saturday night, the janitor asked him why he wasn't at a party. Kevin's response: "Parties will not take me where I want to go."

These athletes had the correct mindset to accomplish what they wanted to accomplish. They learned to say no so they could say yes to their goals and dreams.

This does present a paradox. You are probably saying, "Lighten up, Dennis. Shouldn't I have friends and other interests?" You are asking for permission to have balance and that is a good and healthy response. I like to point out what Katharine Hepburn said one time when asked if she ever was disappointed that she did not have children. The actress reflected and said, "Well, you can't have everything."

I believe that sacrifices are necessary in any human endeavor worth achieving. The challenge is to make the choices, have the right mindset, to accomplish what you want. Business and sports are but a fleeting moment in time. If you want to succeed, go for it. There will be plenty of time for the recreation and fun—which some young people get so immersed in that they lose their moment to shine. Find the balance that works for you, without rationalization. That is the only guidance this book and my thinking can share with you. It is an individual choice. As the old saying goes: Choices have consequences.

So what?
- What are you choosing?
- What are you saying no to?
- What are you saying yes to?
- Do you have the correct mindset going forward?

On Being Fearless

I REMEMBER PLAYING basketball in high school and playing a very good team. We were down by sixteen at half time. In the second half, we came alive, worked our way back, and were up by one point when I got fouled. I was shooting a one-on-one, meaning if I sank both shots, we would win (there was no three-point play back in those dark ages). I made the first one and the opposing coach called time out, an attempt to "freeze" the player by getting him to think about his situation. I still remember my state-of-mind as we walked back on the court with me at the foul line. I heard nothing, I felt nothing, I only saw the rim and when I launched that ball, I knew it was going in. Only then did I hear the crowd and enjoy the moment, a moment that I have enjoyed and can recall forty years later.

That detachment that I felt was, for me, a very healthy response. There was a band playing, the gym was packed with people screaming at the top of their lungs, and all my teammates' efforts were hanging on my performance. Had I thought about any of that, it would have led to a different result I am sure.

Deepak Chopra has written extensively on the topic of successful living. One of the principles he discusses is the principle of detachment. It applies for athletes and business people alike. I believe that is what I experienced in my moment of pressure performance. The principle of detachment is about relinquishing your attachment to the result or the object of your desire. It appears paradoxical to the principle of desire and intent (and the goals that you were encouraged to create). However, Chopra clarifies by saying that attachment creates fear and insecurity. With detachment, there is freedom to create. Great sales people have this ability. If you want the sale too badly, it shows and turns off your prospect. These are great principles to explore and I encourage you to stay curious.[33]

Feel the fear

Everyone feels fear at one time or another. Successful sales people, or athletes, feel the fear and then move on and do what they have to do. It is natural to feel fear. Fear is only part of the rainbow of feelings that we, as human beings, sense. Fear and success are two sides of the same coin. The problem with some is when they feel fear, a chain reaction of emotions sabotage performance. That chain reaction is what you have control over. Control your thoughts (your mindset), and you will control the results.

When failure happens

OK. Failure happens. It is part of life. Did you know that Babe Ruth, the baseball slugger, who held the home run record for years (714 home runs), also struck out 1,330 times? In baseball, if you are successful just one-third of the time at bat, they put you in the Hall of Fame.

Failure is part of life. It is what we do with failure that makes the difference. When playing jazz music, a player will hit a bad note. It is what that player does next that makes all the difference. It is the same with you. Once you fail, what do you do next? Successful sales people get the NO from a customer, and they move on. Hopefully, they are learning from those failures and getting better at the next sales opportunity. The best always learn and move on.

In business, there are great ideas that work commercially and there are ideas that don't make it. Learn and move forward. What mindset do you bring when failure strikes?

So what?
- Failure to learn is learning to fail. Learn how to fail successfully.
- Question to consider: If you had no fear of failure, what would you attempt to do?

Playing to Win

"Know thyself" was the advice of Socrates. Peter Drucker later echoed the same wisdom for business leaders. Enough has been made of this concept that I believe we should officially designate it as a discipline: self-leadership. It is part of the emotional intelligence quotient (self-awareness and self-management). The wisdom in self-knowledge understands the limitations that we put on ourselves. Henry Ford stated, "If you think you can or if you think you can't, you're right."

Our thoughts become our reality. This can lead to sabotage even in the most unbelievable circumstances. Take for example the British Open in 1999. The leader was Jean Van de Velde, a Frenchman who was a 150-to-1 underdog. He was on the last hole and simply needed a six (two over par) to be victorious. To make a long story short, he shot a seven and lost the tournament in a sudden death playoff. This is an example of a breakdown in the mental game, in the mindset.

Years ago, there was a fascinating study of sales professionals at IBM. It showed that the thinking of the sales people predicted their success rate. When someone got an early jump on their sales projections, they slowed down their sales effort as to not exceed their expectations. When sales people were getting close to the end of their sales cycle and they were not at their goal, they would accelerate their sales effort to meet their expectations. This is a great example of how people shape their realities as well as the consistency theory mentioned earlier. There are two forces working here: fear of failure and fear of success.

People understand the fear of failure, but how can someone fear success? Let me ask you this question: What happens when you are successful? If you are in sales, then you have just raised expectations (your own and others). This brings about added pressure and potential self-sabotage.

I was at a senior leadership team meeting for a very successful Fortune 500 company when the team received the results from the last quarter. It was the best quarter in the history of the company. What response do you think I observed in that team when they received the news? There was a collective groan followed by a "how are we going to top that quarter?" mumbling. That team should have been celebrating and slapping high fives like they just won the World Series. But they did not and they soon found themselves in very challenging territory.

I wonder what they then created to match their expectations. Note: I was supporting this client and did not have the rapport or opportunity to debrief this experience with the leader or the team. They were very busy, perhaps too busy to see what they were creating.

On self-fulfilling prophecies

The above is a self-fulfilling prophecy. Many people understand this concept, but like the adolescents and athletes who thought they were invulnerable; people don't seem to take their own thinking too seriously. I am encouraged by the recent books that have appeared on the topic. *The Secret* came out in 2006 by Rhonda Byrne, and then Wayne Dyer followed in 2007 with *Change Your Thoughts, Change Your Life*. A neurologist, Dr. Daniel Amen, had written a book for people that suffered from depression and anxiety entitled *Change Your Brain, Change Your Life*. The message is the same. Your thoughts are the gateway to your reality. If you don't like what you see or what you are experiencing, change your thinking.

Sounds easy enough. It isn't. Or else you would be rich beyond imagination, happy beyond belief, and in great shape. And even if you have all three of these, there is a depth to life that gives meaning and purpose to what you do and who you are. All of these dimensions of life, mind, body, and spirit are accessible through your belief system. Let's move forward.

Permission

Start with giving yourself permission to win, be happy, and be wealthy. Pay attention to what you are saying to yourself. Your self-talk can be revealing. Once you have that healthy mindset, you can move to building the relationships around you.

Relationship power

In business, relationship power is everything. This is your ability to get things done with other people. You need connections in the business world to get things done. How well are you building those relationships? There is another relationship power that is even more important and that is the relationship you have with yourself. That may sound schizophrenic like the old line from a Bill Murray film:

> Roses are red,
> Violets are blue,
> I'm schizophrenic,
> and so am I.

That is making light of a serious subject, but are you OK in your own skin? This has been called self-esteem or self-concept, and it has been largely lost in the business world because the Darwinian model works pretty well. If you don't function well, you get replaced in business (at least in theory). Business did go through a period of entitlement that has been painfully replaced in the past two decades. Today, you need to get good or get out as Peter Drucker suggested in his many writings over the past sixty years. The only person truly accountable for your development is you. Organizations will try to help and many have excellent training programs in place. They are there as catalysts for you. You must provide the spark.

So, how would you rate your relationship with yourself? Listen to others and get feedback from all around you. The Chinese have said there are always three perceptions of ourselves to consider:

1. Self-perception
2. Perception from others
3. The way we truly are

Listening

Here is a lost art in business. There is so much noise in the air these days. Ten thousand channels to choose from and nothing to watch, talking heads everywhere, and eighty-five e-mails an hour to handle. When do we have time to listen? Here is the good news. We only pay attention to a small percentage of the noise around us each day. One neurologist said that we filter out 94 percent of the sensory stimuli received each day. That leaves only 6 percent that we pay attention to! Is it any wonder that we have communication problems in our organizations? We may all be paying attention to a different 6 percent.

On taking action

This is the final step toward creating a healthy mindset. If you have been honest and you know you need to align with a healthy high performing mindset, then it is time to take action. The action should be focused, simple, and measurable. Let people know what you are working on, enlist their support (where appropriate), get a coach to support you, and be painfully honest with your effort and results. The next chapter talks about what is needed to make the action stick.

So what?
- Is your self-talk positive, encouraging, inspiring?
- How is your relationship with yourself?
- How do others see you?
- What mindset are you using to get the results you are looking for?
- What mindset do you need?

On Human Nature and Motivation

EVERYONE IN SPORTS and business is looking for a competitive edge. It is the "magic bullet" that will save a company or a sports team. Sometimes a superstar moment or person or idea can come around and save a company or sports team, but more often it is common individuals who do the uncommon tasks that lead to excellence. The U.S. Olympic hockey team of 1980 is an excellent example. How that team of average hockey players beat the professional team of Russians and the rest of the field is still considered one of the major upsets in Olympic history. Great sales teams are individuals doing uncommonly great things in sales. In business, like in sports, extraordinary things are being accomplished by common people every day. And this is the way it should be as Peter Drucker clearly stated: "If you need geniuses to run your business, you are in trouble."

Outstanding performance can come from common people, but there has to be some form of fire inside the individual that motivates her to perform. Douglas McGregor's Theory X and Y was a prominent theory in 1960.[34] Theory X said the average human being has an aversion to work and will avoid it if she can. Theory Y said that work is a natural part of the human condition much like play or rest. Theory X emphasized a strong command and control manner to get work done while Theory Y suggested a more participative style of management to get work done. What is your attitude toward work? More theory X or Y? If you are more X, then you will need more support and encouragement (direction and control). If you are more Y, then you are more self-contained and autotelic (self-adjusting). Know yourself. Be honest and ask for the support you need to be successful.

How do you see yourself? Ted Williams, the greatest hitter in baseball history, always saw himself as the greatest hitter who ever lived. And here is a quote from Mary Lou Retton: **"Each of us has a fire in our hearts for something. It's our goal in life to find it and keep it lit."**

I graduated many years ago from a small private liberal arts college in western Pennsylvania, and at our baccalaureate Rich DeVoss, a cofounder of the Avon Corporation, addressed us. I still remember his message that day. He said that after we graduate, we will be full of enthusiasm and will want to change the world. That is the first phase of our lives. Then, there will be successive phases where, essentially, our energy and enthusiasm will be challenged. Some may give up on their dreams. His challenge to us was to stay in that first phase as long as we could. I never forgot that message. Motivation comes from the inside out. Environment can help motivate, and some people can say things to motivate you. But in the end, it is you who must allow the flame to grow and energize your performance.

As the song from the 1983 movie *Flashdance* so clearly stated: Take your passion. Make it happen.

So what?
- Where is the fire inside of you?
- Is the flame burning bright?
- Do you need to reignite the fire inside you?
- Don't like what you see or hear? As the old Michael Jackson song suggested, "Take a look in the mirror." What can you change to influence perceptions of you?

The Boiled Frog Awareness

JIM LAHR AND Tony Schwartz, authors of *The Power of Full Engagement*, assert that energy management is even more important in business than time management.[35] I would agree. It is not only motivation that is important in sports or business, but managing your energy in a constructive and effective manner. So what if you are at a meeting or a sales presentation if you are so exhausted that the meeting or presentation is only getting 20 percent of you? What about the family or significant others in your life? Is your life like the executive I was working with who said, "The Company gets the best of me and my family gets the rest of me?" This is not what she wanted. It was not what the company wanted either. It was the way things evolved. This executive had experienced what I like to call "the boiled frog syndrome."

The Boiled Frog Syndrome: If a frog is dropped into a pot of hot water, the frog will jump out and at least try to escape its fate, but if you put a frog in a pot of cold water, and gradually raise the temperature, it will never try to escape and will eventually die in the boiling water. How many people are like this frog or this executive who wake up one day and sees themselves in an unhealthy state?

This boiled frog syndrome is what I referred to earlier as an "unhealthy normal" state. Only upon reflection can this perspective be seen for what it truly is—unhealthy and unsustainable.

Let's say that you are motivated. You have reflected and you have a vision of what you want to achieve. What can keep you going after the motivation wears off? Here are two quotes from the sports world:

"Motivation gets you going. Discipline keeps you going."
—Jim Ryan, world-class miler

"The only discipline that lasts is self-discipline."
—Bum Phillips, former football coach, Houston Oilers

In the business world, there has been strong reference to discipline in great companies and great sales people. Jim Collins referred to great companies having discipline. In his book *Good to Great*, there are twenty-two references and eighty pages about discipline in great companies.[36] Zig Ziglar, Brian Tracy, and Seth Godin have studied successful sales people. They all arrive at similar conclusions about discipline. Successful people have a plan and they work the plan. In spite of sales being so important, sales experiences can be disappointing. Here is a quote from Seth Godin's blog on his sales experience:

> *I arrive at Westchester Toyota and pass two or three salespeople loitering outside. Inside, there were two or three more, sitting in a line of chairs, waiting for the signal from the headmistress at the counter.*
>
> *My guess is that even for a thriving brand like Toyota, most of these guys weren't paid so much. They were "good" salespeople, lifers who showed up, did what they were told and closed a sale here and there.*
>
> *It soon became clear that the salesperson who was assigned to me wasn't "great." The dealership had messed up: He had no record of my appointment, no file, no history of why I came. But he just punted. He made no effort to engage with me or look me in the eye or empathize with my frustration at the complete waste of time my call yesterday had been. He gave up after about ten seconds, bummed out that he had lost his place in line. So I left.*
>
> *Driving home, I started to think about the discontinuity in the graph of salespeople. Discontinuities are interesting, because that's where you can see how a system works. In this case, it's obvious that a great salesperson is going to sell far, far more than a good one. Nine women working together can't have a baby in one month, and ten good salespeople still aren't going to close the account that a great one could. That's because it's not a linear scale. The great ones reach out. They work the phones when they're not first in line. They understand what a customer wants. They're not just better than good. They're playing a totally different game.*

The difference between good and great in sales is huge. The same occurs in sports. One of the reasons that expansion in sports is challenging is that people will not pay to see average talent. This leads us to the Catch-22: drug-enhanced performance. We love to see hitters hit long home runs. I can remember taking my daughters to see Mark McGwire take batting practice. It was a delight to watch those long balls fly off into the distance. Even though he played for the opposition, we cheered for him and wanted to see him perform (even at the expense of the home team).

What about enhanced performance in business? We have seen our share of false sales reports, enhanced P&Ls (profit-and-loss statements), and bogus stock prices that have tainted the business sector and led to a distrust of corporate executives and business people in general. Some of my clients in Big Pharma have said they are tired of defending their corporations as news coverage consistently puts their company in a bad light. Everyone is looking for an edge, yet at what price?

There are four D's that Gary Mack used with athletes that might serve as guidance for you as well:

> **Desire**. As mentioned in an earlier chapter, "want" power is as important as "will" power; what is your dream and how badly do you want it?
>
> **Dedication**. Dedication is turning desire into action (like hitting one-hundred golf balls from the sand); Lou Holtz, the great former coach of Notre Dame, said that dedication keeps you going versus bailing out when the boat starts to leak.
>
> **Determination**. Perseverance, especially when the going gets tough, is a constant staple of the excellent. It is not that winners never quit. That is an old maxim that is only partially true. Winners know when to quit … and that is long after the competition has gone off to the next thing. Again, I like Seth Godin's book, *The Dip*, where he talks about winners knowing when to quit on a bad idea and when to stick with a good idea.[37]
>
> **Discipline**. This is the glue that keeps it all together. This means making the cold calls whether you want to or not, calling on that physician for the one-hundred-and-first time, shooting one-hundred more free throws, or planning your next day. Here is what Tom Landry said, the Hall of Fame coach with the Dallas Cowboys:

"It is not setting goals that are important. It's deciding how you will go about achieving it and staying with that plan. The key is discipline."

Amgen has been one of the most outstanding companies in the past thirty years. In 1980, George Rathmann co founded the biotechnology company. The company provided such consistent returns that as little as $7,000 invested in Amgen in 1983 would have grown to over $1 million in the year 2000.[38] The discipline to produce those results came from Rathmann's experience at Abbott Laboratories where a CFO, Bernard Semler, has instituted what he called responsibility accounting. Every dollar and every idea was tracked rigorously just as investors hold entrepreneurs accountable. This created a *culture of discipline* that Rathmann took with him to Amgen.

So what?
- What is your plan?
- What area of your life might you be "a boiled frog?"
- Do you have the four D's to execute your plan?

Mindset for Success

ATTITUDE IS LIKE a pair of eyeglasses. It is the lens through which you see the world.[39] I can remember Zig Ziglar telling me a story about how a big strike in the automotive world was happening. He was speaking to this group and on one side of him sat a person complaining about the strike and how it was killing his business. The person on the other side of him was telling him how the strike was helping his business (and he encouraged Zig that if he knew a way to keep the strike going a little bit longer to please do so). Zig was astounded to find that both vendors were in the same business. What makes one person see opportunity while another sees nothing but problems? The answer is obvious, isn't it?

On attitude
There are many wonderful quotes on attitude. Here are some of my favorites:

"I am still determined to be cheerful and happy, in whatever situation I may be; for I have also learned from experience that the greater part of our happiness or misery depends upon our dispositions, and not upon our circumstances."
—Martha Washington

"Your mental attitude is something you can control outright and you must use self-discipline until you create a Positive Mental Attitude—your mental attitude attracts to you everything that makes you what you are."
—Napoleon Hill

"Any fact facing us is not as important as our attitude toward it, for that determines our success or failure."
—Norman Vincent Peale

Napoleon Hill, commissioned by the Carnegie Foundation to find out why people were successful has, perhaps, captured the essence of this book. Your attitude will determine your altitude (a good metaphor for climbing the ladder of success) provided your attitude includes a discipline that will point you toward that desire.

Martin Seligman wrote a book, *Learned Optimism,* and based on his work with two professional baseball clubs, the St. Louis Cardinals and New York Mets, he accurately predicted who would win the following season—the NY Mets. Talent being equal, optimism will tilt the odds.

Jim Collins spoke of optimism in the leaders that he saw leading large complex organizations. He referred to this phenomenon as The Stockdale Paradox in reference to Admiral Jim Stockdale and his imprisonment in the "Hanoi Hilton," a prisoner-of-war camp at the height of the Vietnam War. For eight years, he was tortured and lived in a hole in the ground. When asked what helped him survive when so many did not, he said:

"I never lost faith in the end of the story. I never doubted not only would I get out, but that I would prevail in the end and turn the experience into the defining event in my life, which, in retrospect, I would not trade."

Jim Collins pressed on, "Who didn't make it?"

"Oh that was easy," Stockdale replied. "It was the optimists. They would say that we will be out by Christmas and that would not occur, then Easter and that would not occur, then Thanksgiving ... they died of a broken heart."

So, the Stockdale Paradox is the combination of facing current reality (regardless of the pain) and never losing faith that you will prevail in the end.[40] What a great example of a winning mindset!

So what?
- What lens (attitude) are you using to view your world?
- What adjustments do you need to make to achieve a more positive mindset?
- Do you have faith that you are moving toward a better place?

Get Good

SITTING THE BENCH or "riding the pines" is not a fun experience for anyone whether you are in the little league, minor leagues, National League, or business league. Athletes want a chance to prove themselves. Business people want a chance to prove themselves as well. One of the greatest challenges for organizational leadership is to provide constant challenge and growth to all employees. It is difficult. Some do not even try. The result is high turnover, a costly statistic in most cases.

This is an organizational paradox because organizations need to systematize processes and how work gets done, yet keep people engaged and challenged. It is a difficult balance. The organization needs to win most of the time. It is hard to argue with the competitive gain of mass production and systematization. Yet, people make the organization work and people make up the culture, the tangible energy felt in a workplace. In the end, it is this energy that can be a competitive advantage for the organization, for it cannot be duplicated.

So, now we are back to the individual and the mindset of the individual that leads to the culture of the organization. Each person plays a role in the organization just like the players on a team. When you are not playing, you can be improving and working on your skill development.

> "Attitude is a choice. Think positive thoughts daily. Believe in yourself."
> —Pat Summit, women's basketball coach, University of Tennessee

Each person needs to think of themselves as having value for the organization. That value can be determined like a stock exchange quote. Now remember that stocks are more about psychology than economics, so don't think this is about actual numbers. But think about your value and what you are doing. Is it increasing your value or decreasing your value? If an athlete "riding the pine" or a sales person not on a sale is complaining about the business, product, or environment, what has happened to their value to the organization? It has gone down. Use your time wisely. Increase your value. Get good or get out as Peter Drucker said.

Tom Peters, co-author of *In Search of Excellence* written in the early '80s and consultant to many Fortune 500 companies, wrote an article about Brand You and encouraged people to become CEO of Me, Inc. This challenge was offered to all people in organizations and is the business equivalent to raising your stock price. This notion is counterintuitive in the era of the big organization. In some organizations that I worked with, it was very difficult for leaders to talk about what they accomplished because they were conditioned to talk about "we."

I understand the sentiment behind this conditioning, but it doesn't take a rocket scientist to figure out how this thinking can go too far. Back in 1956, William Whyte wrote the book *The Organization Man*. This book was in response to the many large organizations, and the culture that was forming around them. In 2001, Daniel Pink wrote a book called *Free Agent Nation*. Pink was working in the White House and got caught up in the self-importance of it all, became a boiled frog, and went out on his own. He traveled the country and found many people who did the same. If you look at what has happened to sports, with players moving around every few years and a total lack of loyalty to any one team (and the team ownership gladly reciprocating), one can make the argument that business is heading in the free agent direction.[41] One thing is for sure: the contract between employer and employee has changed.

The most effective and accountable thing that you can do is to continue to learn, add competency to your own stock portfolio, and increase your value. This is the healthy mindset that you need, so you are not complaining when your company is sold, when your division is eliminated, or when your job becomes redundant. The change that you see all around will continue to accelerate, only adding to the seemingly unsteady environment. Control what you can control—your own thinking and the value you bring to any organization.

Like a baseball player riding the pine, you can choose to just sit there—or you can study the players and mentally rehearse what you would do. This mental rehearsal can provide the edge you will need to make a difference when you are in the game.

As Gary Mack suggested to players, "It doesn't take talent to hustle and work hard. Invest in yourself with a positive attitude and can-do thinking."[42]

So what?
- When you are not working at your skill, what are you doing? Is it adding value?
- Are you continuously learning?
- Get good or get out.

Believe in Yourself

"The biggest thing is to have a mindset, a belief; you can win every tournament going in."

—Tiger Woods, professional golfer

WHEN TIGER WOODS won his first PGA Championship at the age of twenty, he was asked if he ever in a million years thought he would have achieved this feat at such a young age. His response was not arrogant, but confident and telling of his mental rehearsal and belief in himself. "Absolutely!" was his one-word response.

Several years ago, I did some research on the most successful styles of coaching. I myself was coaching, and I wanted to see what style I needed to emulate to be the most successful I could be. I found out there are many different styles of coaching that are successful. The key ingredient is belief. Each coach must believe in what they are doing. When the team believes in the coach, and the coach believes in his team, there is an energy that develops that turns into momentum. In business, the same energy can develop.

In extensive research on the most effective managers, a Gallup poll surveyed a million people and eighty-thousand managers to find out that people do not leave companies, they leave managers.[43] You have to believe in yourself and in your team. To quote Dick Vermeil, the Super Bowl coach of the St. Louis Rams: **"When you believe in yourself and the people you surround yourself with, you will win something really big someday."**

Aubrey Daniels has written extensively on the topic of getting the most from your people in the business world and he shares the ABC model with business leaders. This tool can help prepare your mind for what is ahead.

> **A – Antecedent or Activating Event.** This could be a tournament or team meeting or your first day on the job.
> **B – Behavior.** This is what you do because of the event or antecedent.
> **C – Consequences.** These are the results of what happens to the performer.[44]

Let's look at some irrational beliefs that people have about themselves that can impede a healthy mindset for peak performance:

- In business, I'm not smart enough.
- In sports, I'm too small, too slow.
- The job is too big.
- If I fail, people won't like me.

And you can probably add your own list of inhibitors to peak performance. These thoughts, these gremlins need to be replaced with positive beliefs to lead to a successful outcome.

Beliefs drive behaviors which drive results. Sales people need to believe in their product and their ability to sell the product. Muhammad Ali, the great boxing champion, said that if you aren't the best, pretend you are. His energy and confidence were contagious.

"Fake it until you make it" was once a saying I disliked. What about being authentic? But later, I understood that this was a game I needed to play with my own mind. It was a healthy paradoxical game that helped me achieve the correct mindset for success. I agree with Ali, the Greatest Showman on Earth. I believe as he was convincing the world, he was convincing himself as well.

So what?
- What about you? What are your beliefs about your ability?
- What about your team? Do you believe in them? Do they believe in you?
- What winning mindset do you need to move forward?

As a Person Thinketh

ONE OF THE classic self-help books is by James Allen, *As a Man Thinketh* (you can download a free copy at www.asamanthinketh.net). The author puts it this way:

> Mind is the Master-power that molds and makes,
> And Man is Mind and evermore he takes,
> The tool of Thought, and, shaping what he wills
> Brings forth a thousand joys, a thousand ills: --
> He thinks in secret, and it comes to pass:
> Environment is but his looking glass.

If an athlete or businessperson is thinking unhealthy thoughts, it is an invitation for failure. This unknowingly and unwittingly destructive process is carried out in the athletic arena, the sales meeting, the community, and the project management meeting. A helpful tool to battle your own gremlins in your mind is a technique from Tim Gallwey. Tim calls it STOP. Here is how to use this acronym to challenge unhealthy thinking:

Step back from what you are doing.

Think about what you are thinking. (Will this thought help me achieve what I want to achieve?)

Organize your thoughts in a more constructive AND realistic pattern. (See the Stockdale Paradox above.)

Proceed. (Take action.)

Golfing is a wonderful sport to test your thinking. Many will approach a hole and see water. The first thought usually is something like, "Don't hit it in the water." But the mind throws out the negative, so the thought that is in your mind is "Hit it in the water." Sure enough, the body complies.

Replace unhealthy thinking with healthy thinking. Many executives that lack confidence in a certain situation need a positive mantra. I was working with a female executive who was highly successful, but was intimidated by an aggressive boss (whom she respected greatly). The respect was mutual, but in conversations with her boss, she would lose her confidence and compromise her stance on a given position (a position that she was usually correct about). Her mantra became a common one used by many over the years: "I am strong and powerful."

If you close your eyes and say this to yourself ten times, you can't help but feel stronger. There are even tests to prove this assertion and much has been written about this research by Dr. David Hawkins, a trained kinesiologist.[45]

Since the mind is not capable of having two dissenting thoughts occupy the same space in your brain, the conflict will be resolved by you filtering out the conflict or accepting it and changing. In psychology, the name of this phenomenon is called cognitive dissonance. The following is a brief description from Wikipedia:

> In simple terms, it can be the filtering of information that conflicts with what one already believes, in an effort to ignore that information and reinforce one's beliefs. In detailed terms, it is the perception of incompatibility between two cognitions, where "cognition" is defined as any element of knowledge, including attitude, emotion, belief, or behavior. The theory of cognitive dissonance states that contradicting cognitions serve as a driving force that compels the mind to acquire or invent new thoughts or beliefs, or to modify existing beliefs, so as to reduce the amount of dissonance (conflict) between cognitions. Experiments have attempted to quantify this hypothetical drive. Some of these have examined how beliefs often change to match behavior when beliefs and behavior are in conflict.
>
> Social psychologist Leon Festinger first proposed the theory in 1957 after the publication of his book *When Prophecy Fails*, observing the counterintuitive belief persistence of members of a doomsday cult.
>
> In popular usage, it can be associated with the tendency for people to resist information that they don't want to think about, because if they did it would create cognitive dissonance, and perhaps require them to act in ways that depart from their comfortable habits. They usually have at least partial awareness of the information, without having moved to full acceptance of it, and are thus in a state of denial about it.[46]

Mental training and mental rehearsal is about aligning your thoughts with where you want to go, your vision. This alignment is not easy or else everyone would be doing it. It requires a discipline, a self-discipline that you have full control of. After Tiger Woods completed one of his PGA victories, he told his father (who was not at this tournament), "I heard you, Pop. I heard your voice telling me to trust my stroke." He sank a tough eight-foot putt to win on the last hole.

So what?
- What are you hearing from your own thoughts?
- What voices are the loudest?
- Are you ready to discipline your own thinking to accomplish what you envision?

Who's in Charge?

ARE YOU SERVANT or master to your emotions? Regardless of IQ, athletes and business people like to be "smart." In business as well as sports, if you do not have control over your emotions, then your emotions will control you. I like the analogy of fire. It can warm you and cook your food, or it can destroy everything in its path. Emotions are energy in motion. Emotions have no feeling and no brain. It is just pure energy. That energy can be used constructively or destructively.

I have been in corporate cultures that allowed screaming and dysfunction to occur in the workplace. The leaders showed everyone how to do it (through their actions), and it became an "unhealthy normal" in that corporate environment. This behavior was not written down in the corporate handbook, but it was obvious it was accepted as part of a "passionate leader." In that culture, if you did not raise your voice, stomp your feet, and throw some vulgarities around, your leadership was questioned.

Tony Dungy is a fascinating leader as head coach of the Indianapolis Colts. He never raises his voice in a sport that is very emotional. Being a former coach myself, I marvel at his ability to control his emotions and never raise his voice. Leaders in business do either of two things: they allow emotions to get out of control or they advocate a more level-headed approach to the daily challenges of business. This concept is known as the Shadow of Leadership, and according to Larry Senn's research and work, organizations are simply the shadow of their leaders.[47]

Once, when I was working with a utility organization in the Midwest, my colleague and I had some bad news for the CEO. Unwittingly, he was fostering a culture of "shoot the messenger." When we approached him with this feedback, news that other senior executives would not share, his first response was, "Who said that?"

We rested our case.

In playing sports, you know that the more you lose control of your emotions, the more you lose control of the game. Business and life is no different since business is just a subset of life.

So what?
- What shadow are you casting on your organization?
- Are your emotions a pump or drain on the energy of others?
- Are you the master of your emotions or a slave to your emotions?
- What discipline do you need to better master your own emotions?
- What is the price for not mastering your emotions?

The FUD Factor

MANY PEOPLE MAKE a good living based on fear (F), uncertainty (U), and doubt (D). The insurance industry exists because of our "FUD Factor." Derivatives, put options, and mutual funds are all financial vehicles that help us diversify and spread our risk, hoping to eliminate FUD.

The absolute worst thing that a business leader can do is worry about failure. The same is true in sports. Accountability is about taking action, not worrying if what you are doing is flawless (flawless in the perfect sense). There are many tough choices that need to be made in business. General Electric had the four E's to GE leadership and anyone who has worked with a GE leader or someone from that leadership factory knows that one of those Es stands for the "edge" to make tough decisions. That is a good quality for any leader to aspire to. Here are the other E's, and they are worth mentioning as you create the right mindset for yourself going forward:

1. Lots of personal energy
2. Ability to energize others
3. The edge to make tough decisions
4. Ability to execute
5. All the Es are tied together with a passion for life and work[48]

These E's are important around the world as country leaders are wrestling with very contentious issues at home and abroad. These E's are important to you as you prepare your mindset for success. Fear is not in the plan and it is a deliberate and disciplined effort to feel the fear and acknowledge its presence, but not let it prevent you from taking action.

Military, police work, and firefighters are good examples of people who need to deal with fear in the proper execution of their work. Business people deal with fear and in a much more subtle manner than these professions. The decisions business people make are critical for the business success, and the fate of many lives and families rest in the result of those decisions. It can create fear, uncertainty, and doubt.

Healthy high performance in sports, in sales, or in leadership is not played well in a state of fear, uncertainty, and doubt. A friend was in a position in a company that marketed its talent management tool and process. However, the management of their own talent was severely lacking and many employees were unhappy. This company was in a state of "unhealthy normal," and my friend was in the middle. Her efforts to align her work with her talent were met with kind words and helpful intention, but no action. Many employees in a similar state may advise her to "play it safe" and keep her head down and this too shall pass. This strategy is often a strategy of employees undergoing massive change efforts. It is exactly the opposite of what leaders and shareholders need from the employee base, but it is a wonderful defense mechanism for anxious employees. FUD is an acronym to avoid, and if you take the first letters of stress, anxiety, and fear you spell SAFE. In football, when a team plays it safe, that is when the opposition usually marches down the field. Playing it SAFE and engaging in stress, anxiety, and fear is anathema to high performance.

I can remember a homecoming football game many years ago in my college days. I was anxious and nervous about the game. We were playing a talented team that would win our division. They had a talented halfback and chances were good that I would be one-on-one with this talent during the game. The stands would be full of alumni and friends. That nervousness is a normal part of any game. That anxiety can be constructive. It helped me prepare for the game and anticipate plays. Many professional sports figures would tell you that if you were not nervous, there would be something wrong. Bruce Jenner, former Olympian, said, "Fear is part of the process. If you weren't scared, you would be in trouble."[49] Usually, the fear and anxiety departs after you engage in the activity. It is only your thinking about the future that creates the anxiety and fear. Before I give you the antidote for stress, anxiety, and fear, take some time to honestly answer these questions.

So what?
- How are FUD and SAFE playing out in your life?
- Do they help or hinder your performance? In what ways?
- What mindset do you need to win?

On Focus

WHEN YOU LIVE in Philadelphia (as I do), and you are around sports as long as I have been (I grew up in Pittsburgh where it seemed everyone played a sport each season), you get familiar with the worst word in performance—choked. The 1964 Phillies are held up as a standard in the ultimate choke performance. Up six games going into the last week of the 1964 baseball season, they managed to lose. But choking is part of life and performance. As many athletes will attest, "We all choke at one time or another." Michael Jordan missed many last-minute shots, Babe Ruth struck out twice as many times as he hit home runs, parents miss great teaching opportunities, and business people miss sales that are right there in front of them.

It is often said it is not what happens to us that counts, but what we do afterward that determines our success or accomplishment.

Many recall and much has been written about the Tylenol tampering in 1982. Seven people in the Chicago area died from bottles of Tylenol laced with a poison. The company, Johnson and Johnson, had a creed in place that was partially credited with helping managers decide the correct course of action. That action by the J&J employees and the organization allowed the sales of Tylenol to resume their pre-scare levels by the end of that same year. When there is a crisis and performance really counts, it is the focus of the people involved that matters. If values or some other anchor is present, that will help the process. Focus is the key.

I knew a partner in a business who was let go, and when I asked him what he was going to do, he did not know. He had two clients that would probably pay him for some coaching. He lived in one of the highest real estate areas of the country. He needed more if he and his family were to stay in the area.

The displaced partner went to see a person who he has trusted over the years and within ten minutes, the advice was given: "You need to focus. You are all over the place!" The partner stared back at the quick diagnosis and replied, "But I was planning on staying for two or three days."

"You can stay for two or three days, but in the end, I am going to tell you the same thing" was the advice compassionately shared.

So, the partner went about focusing on his two clients. He served them well and from that focus came other recommendations that led to fifteen corporate relationships. Now the partner was in a healthy functioning business. The partner could have worried about the future or regret the past, but he did not. He choose to focus on what was here and now.

So what?
- Where do you spend your time? Past? Future?
- When you get under pressure, what changes for you?

Be Here Now

THESE ARE THREE of the most powerful words in the English vocabulary. It is easy to say and hard to do. Gary Mack used to say to his baseball players, "Full head equals empty bat." In other words, if a player went to the plate with his head full of things he needed to do, he was in trouble. An athlete or a salesperson is in flow and performing well when they are not thinking but simply "being."

Larry Senn is a one of the great salesman in the country today, and I had the pleasure of working with him for twelve years. Larry would prepare for a sales call this way: he would read everything he could on the company and the executives, and then he would forget it all and go "be here now" with the executive. He trusted that his preparation would pay off and the right bit of information would come his way when he needed it. He did not have to think about it. It was a good lesson for sales preparation and it is a good lesson for any performance opportunity. Do your homework! Then let it go and be with the person to connect and find out how you can be of service.

Be Here Now was a pamphlet written by Dr. Richard Alpert in 1971. By 1977, the pamphlet was requested enough to be printed in book form and has enjoyed its thirty-seventh reprinting. These simple words are the antidote to choking. If your mind is not on the future or the past, it is in the present, and you are functioning at your best.

Several years ago, a neurologist noticed with concern that CNN had changed their visual protocol. He noticed that when an interview was going on, numbers flashed below the screen and although he was fascinated with the interview, his attention went to the numbers below the screen and he missed part of the interview. He wondered what this multi-tasking was doing to the human brain as we try to process all this information. It is difficult to "be here now" with so many distractions.[50]

I believe organizations should be diagnosed with the same ailments that we give individuals who cannot focus—ADD and ADHD. I also wonder what we are doing to the attention spans of our employees as we condition them to handle a barrage of information.

Have you ever been in a conversation with someone and they were not there? Have you ever been in a conversation and you were not there? How about a sales meeting where nobody was there?

How would you rate yourself with "being here now?" How about at home? How about that next sales appointment?

So what?
- The right mindset is "be here now."
- What do you need to do to exercise that state of mind for you?

Going Fast by Slowing Down

NOTHING IS AS paradoxical as our fascination with speed in business as well as athletics. "First to market" is the mantra used by organizations trying to be fast, but research has shown that second to market can benefit from the mistakes of the first company. In business, the pioneers do get all the arrows, and the second mouse always gets the cheese!

NCAA football has shown over the years that athletes can get bigger (in football, fifty pounds heavier on average over the past thirty years and faster). And businesses have enjoyed the same love affair with size and speed. Businesses will carry on and then someone will decide that the industry needs to consolidate, and mergers and buy-outs occur at a dizzying pace. After a while, the industry is said to have consolidated and a few big giants remain. I often marvel at the psychology on Wall Street versus the economics on Wall Street. Perhaps economics is like physics in that what we observe is one level of reality (similar to classical Newtonian physics), and at a deeper level, it is a whole new world evolving that has a whole different set of rules (like quantum mechanics). At any rate, Wall Street at times seems to have little to do with economics and a lot to do with psychology.

The paradox of speed

I say this is a paradox because we all want to go fast in a physical sense, e.g., first to market or first to the finish line. The challenge lies in the mechanics of going fast. Let's look at what sports performance coaches have found out regarding what it takes to perform at the top level and see if it applies to sales performance or leadership performance. Here are a few quotes to start:

> "Be quick, but never hurry."
> —John Wooden, former UCLA basketball coach

> "To go the fastest in a race car, you must slow down your mind."
> —race car coach to students at racing center

> "The hurrier I go the behinder I get."
> —old saying on my grandma's refrigerator

I have a friend, an SVP of Operations for an energy company, who is a car fanatic. One year, he decided to treat himself to a week at racing school. You can pay for a week's training where you drive real race cars, and they teach you the fundamentals. There were about twelve people in class. The first day everyone was allowed to race around the track, and their times were recorded. My friend was disappointed. His time was the slowest in the class. All week, the coach kept saying the same thing to encourage my friend: "You must slow down to go fast." Fortunately, my friend was a good learner and he wanted to go fast, so by the week's end, he learned the paradoxical trick of going fast by slowing down his thinking. He moved to the head of the class. I wonder how many people in business need to learn the same lesson. How about you? Is your mind racing from one thing to the next? Are you exhausted trying to keep all the balls in the air? Then this section of the book is for you.

One of the exercises I like to do with a group is pair people up with someone their own size and strength. I have them assume the arm wrestling position and give them these instructions:

> In a moment, I want you to play a game. The game is called "score the most points." You score a point when you force the hands to touch your partner's shoulder. You have fifteen seconds to score points. Go!

The game and instructions are designed to get people into action quickly (and I always allow people to opt out if they feel the activity is not safe for them or they have a sore shoulder, etc.). Like life and business, we are forced to act quickly and usually go on auto-pilot behavior. Participants struggle to force their will on their "opponent." Yet, here we are at a teambuilding meeting or leadership conference, and our basic instincts kick in. Compete ... kill the opponent!

I will never forget the comment of a chairman of a large multinational corporation, speaking to his multinational audience: "If I saw my competition drowning, I would shove a hose down their throat." And this was not meant to be humorous. This was a real sentiment that helped this executive rise to the top of a $40 billion company. Later, this executive had a heart attack and died suddenly, and I just couldn't help but think that this competitive fire in his had something to do with the unhealthy state of his arteries.

The question then becomes how do you balance the competitive fire (which is good) with an unhealthy competitive attitude that can affect your own health and the health of those around you? Remember, that competitor today may become your partner tomorrow. With all the merger activity of recent years, that is a distinct possibility for many corporations.

Team spirit and false bravado

What would happen if the home team that you root for suddenly moved to another city? I like the Seinfeld episode where the question is posed: "What if all the players from New York were traded to Boston and all the Boston players were traded to New York? Who would you root for if you were a New York fan?" You probably would respond to the new New York team. Then, Seinfeld concludes, you are rooting for cotton. It is just the uniform, the cotton, that you root for and not the players.

Around the world, riots break out at a soccer game and people die. In Philadelphia, it is difficult to take my kids to a game because of what our fans do to anyone wearing the opposition's colors, and I do mean anyone—men, women, or children. And what are they rooting for? Cotton?

Now, I understand the passion for the home team and rooting for the hometown colors. But there is a place where that passion overcomes logic and becomes what I call false bravado. This occurs in business as well. Some are just concerned with winning as an individual: my career, my sale, my job security. This is natural and part of a survival game. I think Maslow had it right when he developed the hierarchy of needs.

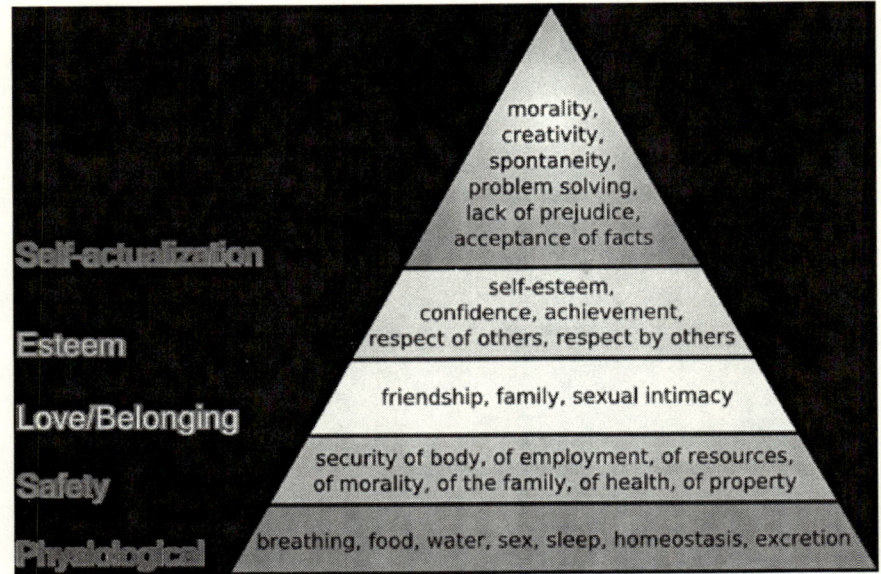

You need to take care of one level of needs before you can move to the next level. In working with executives, I have learned not to worry about them. They are well paid with many options awaiting them (options at many levels!). But the front-line workers with their livelihoods tied up in their job have fewer options (in their minds) and are looking for something different than the leaders. Often, culture-shaping efforts that start at the top, that are well intentioned, are met with cynicism on the front lines. That makes sense when you consider Maslow's hierarchy of needs. The executives are in a different place and have a different perspective.

So, in the spirit of moving fast, executives need to slow down and think about how to best engage the front-line employee. After all, they are the closest to the work, and they have the answers to challenges that the executives may hear about, but haven't experienced. The front line needs to understand and respect the executive perspective. Together, they can do just about anything. It is exciting potential!

Living in Pittsburgh in the '70s gave me an excellent opportunity to see a Super Bowl team and the city fall in love with one another. Pittsburgh Steelers fans are passionate about their team, and one thing is clear to me after all these years: we were and are cheering for cotton! The big picture is that if we go to war, we cheer for the players regardless of what city they came from. When we are handed a project team, we cheer for them regardless of what country they came from.

A healthy mindset understands the immediate passion of a localized team *and* that there is a bigger game to play.

So what?
- How big of a win are you playing for?
- Can you slow down to go fast?

Slowing Down to the Speed of Effectiveness

THERE IS AN interesting story that Gary Mack refers to regarding effort and results:

> Jay Novacek was the tight end for the Super Bowl Cowboys in the '90s and ran track in his college days. One day his track coach told his teammates to run the 800-meter race as fast as they could. They did this and their times were recorded. The next thing the track coach asked the group to do was run the 800-meter race at 90% speed. They did this and their times were recorded.[51]

Guess which times were faster? You got it. The 90-percent times! What is the answer to this? Why were the 90-percent times faster? Here is Gary's response:

> Voluntary muscles are organized into opposing pairs. Running and many other sports are performed most effectively when some muscles are contracting while others are relaxing. Running at top speed, athletes use all of their muscles—the agonists and antagonists. They are accelerating and braking at the same time. The muscles are at odds. This prevents them from running as fast as they can.[52]

How many of us in business are running all out? How many sales people or leaders are trying too hard? Stress and effort still appear to be the red badge of courage that we like to wear in business. How sick can I be and still come to work? This type of loyalty may be appealing to you as a business leader versus the person who disappears at the first sign of adversity, but it is not a healthy high-performing trait. We all know that we need to, at times, put our head down to get through a tough project or timeline, but to constantly ask people to do this day in and day out is unsustainable. It is a train wreck waiting to happen. It is an unhealthy normal.

Teamwork is needed in sports and even more so in business. If a team is working well together, there is an ease and grace that is intoxicating. Like a Super Bowl champion, everyone is in the right position to contribute and do what they do best. They support one another. They coach one another. I remember a Super Bowl Redskins team that the coach, Joe Gibbs, said made it easy. The team coached one another and did what they needed to do. That is the sign of a championship business team. They know what they have to do and they do it. They are self-disciplined and they discipline one another.

How does your team match up against these traits of self-discipline? What can you do to better prepare your own mindset for healthy high performance?

So what?
- Take a sincere look at your work. Are you dedicated to the work?
- Are you committed or just going through the motions?
- What mindset are you operating with? Describe your thinking.
- Are you redlining your engine (working too hard)? What are you running from? Can you slow down to the speed of effectiveness? What would that look like?

PART THREE: ON TAKING ACTION

Observe

"You can observe a lot by watching."

—Yogi Berra

When Yogi Berra said this, he was irritated at his players in the dugout who were not paying attention to the ballgame in the field.[53] Many times, we are not paying attention to what is going on in our own fields. Once in a lifetime opportunities happen everyday and it is only the people who are observing that have the eyes to see.

Business and inherent busyness rewards the action-oriented person. This is important, but the other side of the coin is observation, reflection, and doing nothing. Once we had a Fortune 100 leadership team away for three days on a retreat. The stock of this company went up three dollars while the team was away and disengaged from the business. The joke and half truth that surfaced was that the team was not there to mess things up. Sometimes the best leadership action is non-action, a tough concept for some corporate leaders to understand when they have spent a lifetime doing.

What about sales? Isn't that about doing? Sales people need certain energy and promoting instinct about their product and placement of their product. Yet Zig Ziglar, one of the most prolific sales and motivational speakers of all time, gives this advice in a recent publication:

> Take time to be quiet ... it is during these times that your best ideas will surface ... take a walk with a spouse or significant other and ask them for their thoughts on a topic you have been struggling with. You will be surprised at what insights they can lead you to."[54]

There is so much noise in the business world today that people learn to simply disbelieve what they hear as empty promises. Who you are speaks so loudly. What is on your inside, your character makeup, will determine where you go in this life. Take time to nurture and discipline that internal mindset to be the most successful person you can be. To get that perspective, you will need to become an expert observer.

Observation in sports is about focus. Did you see *The Legend of Bagger Vance*? The director, Robert Redford, did an excellent job of portraying observation when he had the golfer, played by Matt Damon, "in the zone." It was just the golfer, the ball, and the hole. Everything else went away: the people, the noise, and the distractions. That movie was a great example of flow in human performance, and it was a great metaphor for effective self-leadership.

Gary Mack used an exercise to help athletes focus. He would ask them to observe a baseball, golf ball, or basketball (whatever their sport). Then, when their mind started to wander, he would ask them to refocus. I was in a leadership session in Scotland once when a participant said that his father used to take him to the ocean and sit on a big rock. He would tell his son, "Listen to the rock." Gary and this participant were asking the same thing: focus, be present, this is the moment you have now. Don't waste it. You have the same challenge. There is lots of noise all around you every day.

So what?
- Are you observing?
- Are you present?
- You *can* learn a lot just by observing.

Preparation for the Winning Mindset

"The desire to win is useless without the desire to prepare."
—Gordon Wood, 396 wins as a Texas high school football coach

"Chance favors the prepared mind."
—Louis Pasteur

"Luck is when preparation meets opportunity."
—Seneca, Roman philosopher

THE ABOVE QUOTES have been used in a variety of fields. Having the right mindset for accomplishment is a discipline. Practicing for that moment is what *The Winning Mindset for Leadership* is about.

My daughters play basketball, and when they were small, I would go to the games and watch. These energetic athletes would run around the basketball court, and when someone would throw the ball toward the basket, occasionally it would go in. The look of surprise would come over their face and smiles of delight beamed from parents, coaches, and players. As they matured as players, the surprise faded and they expected the ball to go in. This is how confidence develops.

When athletes are asked, "What is the most important part of the mental game?" their answer is always the same: confidence.[55] When I recruited athletes for a football program at a Division 2 college in western Pennsylvania, I always looked for a combination of athletic ability, intelligence, and confidence. There was a fine line between confidence and arrogance. I still look for that same combination in effective leaders in business today. The names are slightly changed: talent, emotional intelligence, and confidence/humility.

Talent. Raw ability; everyone has some gift. What talent has been displayed, what potential exists?

Emotional Intelligence. The best determination of success in any field, Daniel Goleman wrote extensively about this in his past two books, *Emotional Intelligence* and *Social Intelligence*.[56][57]

Confidence/Humility. This blend is a winner mindset. It is great to have confidence (it can overcome a lack of pure talent) coupled with humility (see the Stockdale Paradox earlier mentioned). The world is too complex for any one person to know it all. Shared leadership or distributed leadership is the key to successful work in large, complex organizations or large, complex lives. Confidence and humility make shared or distributed leadership work.

This whole idea of shared leadership or distributed leadership is another book in itself. The bottom line is that control is a myth—at least a myth in the way most people understand it. In business, Peter Block has stated that if the variables are under your control, you are managing. If the variables are not under your control, then you are leading. Sales opportunities are a great microcosm for this dynamic. A salesperson can present the facts and make the pitch, but they cannot control if the person will buy. That control lies with the individual. The salesperson can only influence what the decision will be. That is leadership. Preparing for that opportunity is management, or self-management: studying the product, understanding the client, connecting, balancing confidence with humility, and keeping proper perspective and integrity intact.

The journey to this awareness has been captured by people many times. Most take a lifetime to figure it out. Some never do. The bottom line is to be in the game and totally aware. That awareness will keep you curious and exploring new insights along the way.

The bottom line: The best athletes and the best business people use their mind to program their bodies. Change management programs abound that are unsuccessful. One of the challenges of taking on change is that change has to be an inside-out phenomena. Human nature has a tendency to resist outside force to change.

So what?
- Are you resisting the changing forces around you?
- Are you aware of the changing forces around you?
- How can you best program your own mind for the challenges ahead?

Trusting Yourself

ARE YOU COMFORTABLE in your own skin? I had a brilliant friend who liked to say, "I can only take myself in small doses." This always invoked some humor and self-deprecation. I believe most people think if they are tough on themselves, then others' criticism may not seem so bad. I am not sure, but I have found that athletes and business people are tougher on themselves than most people would be with them. What constructive feedback could I give to my friend when he has insulted himself like that? Perhaps it is a defense mechanism that people use to safeguard themselves against a harsh public. Whatever the reason, we need to become comfortable in our own skin and know who we are with all the blemishes. We must train hard and trust that the time put in will have us prepared when the challenge comes.

The 2000 Masters was won by Vijay Singh. On his bag, before he started his final round, he found a note from his nine-year-old son. It read, "Poppa, trust your swing."

When you trust yourself, you are free. When you have a list of to-do's that you need to check off before you play or while you are playing, you are not free. Being in the zone is about freedom. Trusting yourself is about being free.

If you feel you need to look good in a presentation, you are not free. If you feel you cannot embarrass yourself, you are not free. There are millions of people in organizations who are not free. They are tethered to the culture of the organization that is telling them how they need to be. Your challenge is to keep your own identity while learning the game of the organization—and this not selling out or sucking up as my kids might say. This is about being aware of the mindset you need to be successful and trusting yourself—two compatible ideas and concepts.

So what?
- Do you trust yourself?
- Do you know what it takes to be successful in your organization?
- Have you cracked the success code at your organization? Who has?

Flow

NOTHING IS MORE pleasurable than to have preparation meet with opportunity, and for you to experience what Yuri Vlasov, a Russian weightlifter, called a white moment:

> At the peak of tremendous and victorious effort while the blood is pounding in your head, all suddenly becomes quiet within you. Everything seems clearer and whiter than before, as if great spotlights had been turned on. At that moment you have the conviction that you contain all the power in the world, that you are capable of everything, that you have wings. There is no more precious moment in life than this.[58]

One academic has spent most of his life trying to understand this state in human beings. His book, *Flow*, was his attempt to bring his research to the reading public. I found early in his book a subsection called "The Shields of Culture." It seemed an appropriate warning for today's individuals living in organizations and in countries that may be shielding as the author describes:

> Over the course of human evolution, each group developed its myths and beliefs to deal with the precariousness of its survival ... one of the major functions of every culture has been to shield its members from chaos, to reassure them of their importance and ultimate success ... without such trust in exclusive privileges, it would be difficult to face the odds of existence.[59]

Life is serious. Life is terminal. None of us is going to get out alive. Doesn't it make sense that organizations would evolve with the above purpose and intent? So with all the good intentions, organizations have been around for a long time. But the protection from chaos is a game that can only be played, never won.

It used to be that ballplayers would play on one team for their careers. Business people used to do the same. There was a reciprocal agreement that if someone worked for the organization for a period of time, they would be taken care of later in life (when the chaos would take over). This agreement has undergone a transformation in sports and in business.

Today, star performers move around taking the best deal. The average college graduate today may work at fourteen different careers before they retire into the chaos. As Daniel Pink describes in his book, we are becoming a free agent nation.[60]

All the more reason to best understand the mindset needed to succeed today. The promise of lifetime employment is a false promise. The chaos will come, like it has to hundred of thousands of employees over the years in business and sports. I believe what we have witnessed in sports and in the entertainment disciplines are microcosms for the average business person to learn from. When your usefulness to the organization is no longer seen as useful, you will be let go. When you are seen as useful, you will be retained. The objective for individuals today is similar to the athlete: make yourself useful and/or indispensable to the organization. As Peter Drucker coached for years, "Get good or get out."

These are the cold, hard facts, the chaos that we all want to be protected from. Organizations try to do the job, but the best mindset is to understand the underlying reality. It helps you be the best you can be in the moment while understanding the ensuing chaos.

So what?
- Are you improving each year?
- What are you doing to increase your value?
- Have you had *flow* happen to you or "white moments?"

Overthinking

"I haven't had a streak like this ever in my career," complained a partner at a major consulting firm. He had not sold a big project for one year. He was in a slump. Everyone can get in a slump, a time when they are out of synchronization with the way they like to operate. It can happen to a person at work, at home, mentally, physically, or spiritually.

When a salesperson is in a slump, they usually try to think their way out of it. A baseball player does the same thing. I can remember watching Barry Bonds as a Pittsburgh Pirate having a terrible slump at the worst time, the playoffs. When he finally hit a double, after a zero for twenty-two slump, I could read his lips as the camera caught him dusting himself off, "Finally, it's over."

"Performance is a roller coaster," said Gary Mack. We all have ups and downs. Sales numbers will go up and down. How do we end a slump? The answer is frustratingly simple and illusive.

"That was a great shot," a friend once said when we were shooting around a basketball court. He was a big man and had terrible form and was looking to get a better jump shot. I was two years younger and everything seemed to go in. I would have streaks like that when I couldn't wait for my next shot because I knew it was going in. My friend, with the best intentions, got me thinking about my shooting. He even mentioned that my tongue was hanging out when I shot and was I concerned about that. You can guess what happened. I went through a period where I couldn't hit anything. I was thinking too much.

When athletes get into slumps, they try all kinds of different ways to exit the slump and get back in the groove. Some are superstitious and try certain routines. I remember hearing one coach taking all the bats to a preacher to be blessed with holy water. He returned and told the team this, and that night the team broke the slump by scoring fifteen runs and having twenty-two hits. When newspaper reporters heard of this, they could never confirm if the coach actually did this or if there was a preacher willing to bless the team bats. The fact was the team believed the bats were different that day and it broke the slump.

Michael Jordan, the former NBA star, was once asked about the new players who were getting into people's faces and trash talking.

Michael wisely replied, "I don't want to get in your face. I want to get into your mind." The key is the mindset that you have.

Mindset is an inside-out phenomenon and has nothing to do with outside circumstances. Pressure is a concept that we create in our own little worlds, in our own little heads. Sure, it may look pressure packed to a sports audience and players can get caught up in the moment and become distracted. But performance is based on what is going on in the playground between your ears. The same is true in business or at home with your family. At this writing, I have two daughters at home, and there are many cases of their thinking being tied to performance, and my thinking being tied to their performance.

Performance appears to be reducible to two words: discipline and confidence. Discipline is taking the talent that you have and making sure you are in shape and can perform. Confidence is knowing that you have what you need inside of you to achieve the goal and persevere through adversity. A team can have discipline as well as an individual. Jim Collins talked about disciplined thought, disciplined action, and disciplined behavior in his book *Good to Great*. This separated the good companies from the great companies. It is true for athletes as well.

So what?
- What discipline do you need for your success?
- What do you need to do to improve your confidence in accomplishing your goals? Coaching point: keep it simple.

Paradox and Performance

THIS IS THE most challenging concept for athletes and business people to grasp—paradox. Particularly in Western culture, we like linear explanations. The English language is a reductionistic language, meaning we take a big concept and attach a word to it. Attaching this word makes us feel as if we can, at least, define the concept and have some understanding. Of course, we have only scratched the surface of understanding.

Why do we park in driveways and drive on parkways? Why do we have to slow down to go fast? When we learn something new, why do we need to get worse before we get better? Absurdity seems to be part and parcel to accomplishment and understanding. Is there anything more absurd than the human condition?

One of my favorite books is *Management of the Absurd* by Richard Farson. The book is all about people and the absurdities of the human condition. Farson comments that as long as there are people congregating in organizations, there will be absurdity.[61] People will lead to the greatest disappointments and, conversely, they will lead to the greatest triumphs. Energy is everywhere and potential is everywhere. Constructively focusing that energy and potential is the power of your mindset.

Tiger Woods changed his golf swing after winning a major PGA golf tournament, by one of the largest margins ever. When do you think you are best prepared to make a major change? Some companies and individuals choose to do this when they are at their peak or from a position of strength. Others wait until there is a dire emergency and often do not have the time, resources, or strength for success.

Paradoxical truths

Life, business, and sports are forever changing. There is a saying that captures paradox very well: "The more things change the more they seem to stay the same." A Native American saying goes, "You never step in the same stream twice." Both statements have an element of truth and wisdom.

In one of the great upsets in sports, Muhammad Ali defeated George Foreman by using a rope-a-dope strategy where he let Foreman punch himself out. This was an unheard of strategy and counterintuitive—

paradoxical in nature. New financial instruments are being used every year in business, some too creative and down right illegal, while others are truly innovative and game changing. Business will never be the same. Good business people need to adjust to an ever-changing world. At the same time, some things never change.

Here's an exercise I do with groups: Fold your arms and notice which arm is on top; now fold your arms the other way with your other arm on top. How does that feel? Shake your arms out and fold them again. Which way did you fold them? Probably the first way, and that is what we do as human beings and organizations. We resist change and do things the way we always have. But reality is always changing and moving away from us. At some point, we or our organizational practice is out of sync with reality. We have to adjust—to change.

Here are some other paradoxes to consider:

1. We are all unique; we are all the same. Organizations feel they are different, yet they are similar to other organizations. People are different, yet follow similar patterns of needs and desires. Groups feel they are different, yet go through the same stages of development
2. Less is more. Medicine can work at a certain dosage, but too much can be toxic. Exercise is good to a certain point, but too much results in overtraining and actual weakening of the muscles. Everyone is on a diet, but extreme diets can be lethal. I like the wisdom in the Will Rogers diet: moderation in everything and don't miss a thing.
3. Organization/entropy. Life is neatly organized for us. The year is organized into months, weeks, and days. The days are organized into twenty-four hours. Our work is organized into packets (although technology has helped us blur those packets). Energy is even organized into packets (quanta). Then there is entropy, the idea that as things are organized, there is a force (entropy) that has it falling apart. Have you ever marveled at the organization of a business plan only to see forces go to work that makes it fall apart? I often wonder if our job as project managers, parents, or leaders isn't about just keeping things together, i.e., fighting entropy.
4. The harder you try, the more illusive a goal can be. The "Flow" section discussed this. The Law of Detachment states that to have something, you must detach from the desire to have it—paradoxical, isn't it?[62]

5. Ease and grace can be hard. The promise that I heard years ago was that for everything that you need to do, there is an easy and graceful way to do it. This flies in the face of no pain, no gain that many athletes and business people grew up with.
6. Simplicity and complexity. As life and business become more complex, leaders need the ability to see the simplicity and communicate that simplicity effectively. Willie Mays, the great San Francisco Giant baseball Hall of Famer, once simplified baseball to the following: "When they hit the ball, I catch it; when they throw the ball, I hit it." Simple.
7. Gaining control by giving up control. This is one of the greatest paradoxes of all time. Control comes only after there is surrender to the process. Baseball pitchers that try to aim and steer a thrown baseball struggle to throw a strike. Business leaders that try to control the people and mechanisms of their organization are soon frustrated. Malcolm Gladwell spoke of this element when he discussed the leadership of a retired officer and his success at maintaining command and giving up control—a brilliant and effective leadership strategy.[63]
8. Slow down to go fast. This was discussed earlier; Jay Novachek ran faster at 90-percent effort in track. Prepare and practice, then let it go while performing, and let the moment flow. Sounds goofy unless your have been in a flow state.
9. Fear of failure attracts failure. This is the ultimate paradox in sports, business, sales, and well … life. Your thoughts attract what you are thinking about. This can appear to be almost mystical. It is well-documented in *The Secret*.
10. Prevent Defense (playing it safe can be dangerous). Mentioned earlier, a prevent defense is an invitation to score for the other team. Playing it safe equals danger.
11. In order to go forward, you need to step back. Reflection may be one of the ultimate paradoxes in business, where speed is the mantra.
12. Getting what you want means letting go of what you want. Here is great advice for the business strategists: give yourself permission to win, but then let go of the idea of winning and focus on execution.[64]
13. To find yourself, you must lose yourself. Athletes and world-class business people lose their conscious mind when they are in the zone. They are living "in the moment."

The ideal mindset for understanding much of success is comprehending paradox and its natural presence. Getting worse to get better is only one example.

So what?
- What paradox exists that you are having difficulty with?
- Can you let go to allow a flow into your performance?

Performance Choice

WHAT SEPARATES A good salesperson from a great one? What separates a minor league player from a major league player? What separates good from great? It is the same answer ... consistency. The difference between good and great is sometimes only slight. The Hall of Fame hitter gets one more hit per ten times at the plate versus the average hitter. It is all about consistency. A PGA golfer needs to be consistent through an entire round of golf—four days of consistency to win. A business leader or salesperson needs to be consistent throughout the years to be effective. "Whatever your job, consistency is the hallmark," said Joe Torre, former manager of the New York Yankees. Jim Collins noted the consistent performance of Level 5 leaders in his work on leadership and great companies. In order to be considered great, performance had to be above the norm for your industry and marked over a fifteen-year period.[65] Over that period of time, there were bad quarters and bad days, but it is on those days that leaders distinguish themselves. Jack Nicklaus, one of the greatest golfers of all time, called it "learning how to play badly well." You will have bad days, but can you learn to do badly well?

As mentioned earlier, Peter Drucker, the dean of business management, stated that if you need geniuses to run your business, you are doomed. Business needs to be kept to the simplest elements. Leaders see through complexity to the simplicity on the other side. Can you cut through the complexities in your own life to see the simplicity on the other side?

Human beings have the innate ability to make the simplest elements very complex. Look at the regulations that have plagued business leaders for years. Look at the politicians and how they complicate bills with thousands of special provisions to serve their own constituency's needs. There are examples all around us of complexity desperately in need of simplification.

What are you doing to complicate your own life? Can you simplify?

There was a story of a mountain climber who went to Nepal to climb. As he laid his equipment out in front of him, the sherpa (guide) asked if all the equipment made him happy. "What do you mean?" the climber asked, "I need this to climb the mountain." "No," replied the sherpa, "all this is not needed."

I wonder how much stuff we believe we need to climb the ladder of success only to find that we can travel much lighter.

So what?
- What beliefs and complexities are you carrying around that only make your climb more challenging?
- Can you simplify your life?

The Inner Edge

THE MINDSET OF a champion is a competitive edge. It cannot be duplicated. It can be imitated, but the wonderful fact about human nature is that we are all unique. Yet, as discussed in the paradox section above, we are the same and have similar needs and wants.

Sports have goals and time-defined seasons. Business has goals and time-defined quarters and annual reports. Life has a time-defined cycle as well (your lifespan). How well are you managing your time and energy?

It is worth repeating that performance is not just time management, but energy management. Remember the executive who said, "The organization gets the best of me, and then my family gets the rest of me"? This is not a sustainable or healthy choice. Inner excellence is about a healthy mindset that leads to excellence in all dimensions of your life.

Sure, there will be times when you need to focus and make sacrifices. Andre Agassi made it back to his championship form by focusing on his tennis. Michael Jordan spent hours upon hours of practice to hone the skill and talent that he was blessed with. Like a pendulum that swings consistently back and forth, inner excellence knows when to persevere and when to surrender one need for another greater need.

Inner excellence goes beyond external circumstances. Bill Russell, as mentioned earlier, spoke of the heat of competition and when the team is in this rhythm of competitive fire, it did not matter who made the next great play, it was beautiful to compete and even winning and losing became secondary to the performance. So, what is inner excellence? What are the pointers to this internal quality that can help guide human performance?

Inner excellence is being in tune with the seven forces and seven C's mentioned previously. "All roads lead to Rome" was the saying in Roman times. Excellence has only so many paths to travel as well. Here are some other paths to consider and their connection with the seven forces and seven C's:

- **Vision.** What will success look like when you get there? Does this vision draw you toward the future so you can't wait to get there? Part of the performance force is having a vision.

- **Commitment.** There are only a few major commitments you can make in your life. Be honest with yourself. Are you committed? Are you willing to put some other needs aside while you work toward this vision? The change force is at work here when you put your commitment energy into a vital few versus a trivial many. Focus.
- **Responsibility/accountability.** What more can you do to accomplish your vision? This is an inside-out virtue and cannot be forced from the outside. The performance force is at work here as well.
- **Continuous learning.** Are you willing to adjust along the way? Life is never linear. How can you apply new learning to accelerate your plan in reaching your vision? The paradox force is at work anytime there is learning taking place because truth shrouds itself in paradox.
- **Optimism.** Where are you now? (Be realistic.) Never lose faith that you are moving in a positive direction toward your desired state (your vision). This is part of the presence force.
- **Confidence/humility.** This is the wonderful blend of belief in yourself and your vision with the humility that there are forces far beyond your control at work in the universe. The presence force is at work here as well.
- **Emotional control (EQ).** Know yourself, manage yourself, know others in your social environment, manage those relationships (you are what you eat and you catch what you hang around with). Are your emotions under your control or do your emotions manage you? The relationship force discussed the presence of EQ.
- **Adversity quotient.** Do you believe? Can you face the obstacles that will be thrown in front of you?
- **Character.** The important thing here is to have character and not be one. What values determine your behavior? Write them down.
- **Persistence and patience.** "Nothing can resist the relentless pounding of a hammer." Can you persevere and do you have the patience to accept that what you strive for may not come in the timeframe you had in mind?

Working on the inside shows on the outside. As Emerson stated, "What lies ahead of us or behind us is of small consequence to what lies inside of us."

As the current Gatorade commercial asks, "Is it in you?" Every performance quality can be bucketed in one of the seven forces and seven C's. Master these forces and you can master your potential.

So what?
- What do you need to better discipline your internal mindset?
- Are you putting in the time to prepare?
- Are you mastering the skill needed to perform well?
- What areas from the list above do you need to work on to improve your inner excellence and alignment with the seven forces?

The Hero's Journey

"It is not the size of the dog in the fight, but the size of the fight in the dog."
—an old saying that I heard as a child that has stuck

At five-foot-seven and 155 pounds, I was not an imposing figure on the baseball diamond, basketball court, or football field. I did have a competitive fire in me and I loved watching the little guy be successful in sports. I remember Freddie Patek, a five-foot-four shortstop for the Pirates and Mugsy Boagues, a five-foot-three guard in the NBA.

I am not unusual in the sense that I like to cheer for the underdog, in business as well as sports. Also, I get angry when I see someone bullying a smaller or weaker being, organization, or community.

The Hero's Journey appears many times in human history. Joseph Campbell captured the essence of the journey this way:

- An awakening (illumination, discomfort, pain) resulting in the call to adventure
- A push forward into the unknown (fear, uncertainty, doubt, and hardship)
- Seeking of a mentor
- A series of tests pushes us to the brink (a supreme ordeal)
- We slay the dragon/face the darkness/create meaning, thus drawing out our potential
- Await the next call to adventure

Sports and business provides a setting for all this drama to unfold. It is an appropriate metaphor for accomplishment and a microcosm for success. Although not all athletes can make it in the business world and business people may not make it in the sports world, there are parallels.

Business likes to tell the tale of a person like Horatio Alger, a rags-to-riches story that serves as a story of hope for many immigrants crossing the Atlantic looking for a new start. Sports tell similar tales, like Kurt Warner bagging groceries and later quarterbacking the St. Louis Rams to a Super Bowl win.

In reality those overnight successes have been a story in the making for ten to fifteen years and more. The mindset that created these great performances was started long before their moments of fame.

So what?
- What mindset do you need to prepare for your moment of fame?
- Can you see yourself being the success that you envision?
- Make that vision as real and vivid as possible.

On Playing to Win

WHAT IS THE most important component in business or sports that leads to success? Many business leaders that I have coached and worked with will say something about integrity. If you get results, but you had to cheat to get them, it is considered unfair and illegal. Many leaders work with their organizations on emphasizing values that include customer service, integrity, teamwork, and accountability—high performance values that help achieve ethical results for the organization.

Today, professional sports are mired in controversy over steroid use and other illegal activity. Business has had its fair share of unethical behavior as well. It is clear that if anyone cheats to get results, then the accomplishment is nullified. Yet business leaders continue to look for the silver bullet or easy way to achieve results.

If you really want to look at where kids learn their values, go to any little league game and watch the parents of these ten year olds. I believe true emotional intelligence is measured on these fields, and that we should not look in the field but look in the stands to see what our children are learning. These kids will take these lessons into the business world and into their college careers as athletes.

What does it take for you to be ready for your performance? Athletes prepare in a variety of ways to be ready for their challenges. The important thing to know is what mindset you need to be successful and get yourself ready for your competitive moment.

A CEO prepares for a meeting with analysts on Wall Street. A lead director prepares for a difficult meeting with a struggling CEO. A sales representative prepares for a presentation, and the tough questions need answers. A clerk readies for the onslaught of customers who are in a hurry and all demanding attention and first-class service. These collective mindsets will be ready by default or design—the choice will be up to each professional.

Our brains are like our handedness; we have a tendency to use them in certain ways. However, there are probably an infinite number of ways to actually engage the brain and all its capabilities.

So what?
- Do you know how your brain functions?
- What are your strengths?
- What do you seem to do well?
- What are your challenges and how can you best prepare for your competitive moment?

The Contest

THE CONTEST IS serious business. My roommate and I use to listen to Jethro Tull when we were preparing for a college football game. Some locker rooms are full of music as teams prepare. Other people need quiet to reflect and play the game in their heads. This mental preparation is getting into the mindset needed for successful performance.

Business people need successful mindsets as well. Some people are working in very unhealthy environments, and they know they need a different mindset to just survive the day. Some people do this so many times that they start to believe this is normal. This leads to the boiled frog syndrome that we discussed earlier. Whatever the routine, business people use rituals to prepare for the day, like most athletes. The question is what is your routine?

Some people like to joke around and some like to focus. Respect each others' preparation and find what works best for you. I have found that the best mantra is to take your job seriously, but take yourself lightly. This can help you find a healthy balance between the intensity of preparation and ease of performance.

The cubic centimeter of opportunity

In business, people seem to value busyness. This is true in sports as well. When I was a Division 2 football coach, I was told that when I walked through the hotel lobby, I was supposed to walk with intensity and purpose. This was to mimic being in a hurry and very busy.

A funny story relayed by Hal Hunter, a former professional and college football coach, was about his preparation for a game with Kentucky. Hal used to work at Kentucky, but now he was at Indiana. He kept calling the athletic office at Kentucky the week before their big game. If someone answered late at night, he told the staff to keep working (after all, they were still in the office at Kentucky). Game day arrived and Indiana did win. Hal was meeting with people he knew at Kentucky, and he ran into the janitor. "How are you doing?" Hal asked.

"Fine," said the janitor, "except somebody kept calling last week when I was trying to sweep up the office."

I wonder how many people are trying to "look busy" in business and life, just like the athletic examples mentioned above? Do we really need the stress and effort present in the business world today?

On game day, you can be prepared and still have a balanced life with priorities clear and your focus where it needs to be.

So what?
- What is your routine to prepare?
- What are you making up to appear busy?
- Could you better balance your life if you told yourself the truth?

Your MBS Degree and the Mirror Test

BEFORE MICHAEL JACKSON received such negative publicity for his life offstage, I liked to refer to his hit, "Man in the Mirror." It was a great accountability song and the place to look when you are not getting the results you want in your profession or athletic career.

How are you playing the game? There is a great saying that captures this question well:

> When the Great Scorer comes to write against your name,
> It is not whether you won or lost,
> But how you played the game.

In sports as well as business, we have come to worship the winner. Yet, it is sometimes the fallen that are the true winners. There are a few quotes to help those who feel they are down. First, one from Kahlil Gibran, the Lebanese poet who described joy and sorrow this way:

> The more sorrow carves into your heart,
> The more joy it can contain.

The second one is from Thomas Edison, when asked how it felt to fail in ten-thousand experiments before finding the right material for the filament in a light bulb:

> It was a 10,000 step process in finding the right filament for the light bulb.

I like the definition of success that I received from John Wooden, the UCLA basketball coach Hall of Famer. It hangs in my office as a reminder:

> Success is peace of mind which is a direct result of self-satisfaction in knowing you did your best to become the best that you are capable of becoming.

He also repeated a poem that I still remember to this day, thirty years after hearing it:

> A careful man I want to be
> A little fellow follows me.
> I do not dare to go astray,
> For fear that he'll go the self-same way.

Many sports figures and business figures today would not pass the mirror test. Many have ruined their lives with alcohol and drug abuse, domestic dysfunction, and general spiritual bankruptcy. I like to remind myself and others about the basics:

> **Mind.** Like a garden, are you cultivating a healthy harvest?
> **Body.** This is the only vehicle that you get in this life; are you taking care of it?
> **Spirit.** Do you believe there is something beyond you?

I call this the MBS degree. Once you have all three of these dimensions developed in your life, you are best prepared for a mindset that will lead to sustainable healthy high performance. By attending to these dimensions, you will be building a great foundation for your professional and personal success.

A Harvard study focused on what made a life successful. Here are the results of that study and what they eventually called the five L's[66]:

1. **Love.** Many great minds have stated that the only need humans have is to love and be loved. Yet in business and in politics, it is uncomfortable to talk about love without drawing laughs or an HR warning. All your work and play should involve love and feeling about what you are doing.
2. **Labor.** Sigmund Freud supposedly said on his deathbed that all that matters is love and work. Human beings love to work and accomplish things. My definition of success has always been: do work that you love … and get paid for it. Then you will never go to "work" ever again.
3. **Learn.** We should all be continuous learners who constantly are curious about how the world works. Yet, judgmental criticism is common and seen as part of the business and athletic landscape. There is a better way! Learn and move forward.
4. **Laughter.** Norman Cousins cured himself of cancer by

renting Laurel and Hardy movies, the Three Stooges, and the Marx Brothers. You should be laughing on a daily basis. How are you doing?

5. **Leave, Let Go.** As Richard Leider has said, "We need to unpack our bags (our internal beliefs) and travel lighter." It turns out that forgiveness is not only a good spiritual value, but it is a success value as well. How good are you at forgiving and letting go of past harms, bad relationships, and hurtful memories?

Jim Abbott played major league baseball with one arm; one of the top motivational speakers has a severe case of cerebral palsy. He tells the audience, "I have cerebral palsy. What's your excuse?" Failure is always temporary. Learn from failure and move on.

So what?
- What mindset do you meet failure with?
- What do you do next?
- Do you have your MBS degree?
- Rate yourself on the five L's above on a scale from one to ten. How did you do?

The Big Win in The Big Picture

THE BIG WIN does not show up on the front page of the newspaper. The big win happens in one million different ways on a million different occasions. There are six billion people on this earth, and the ones who get their story told in the media are few indeed. The big win is the relationships that you nurture along the way, the people you help achieve their dreams along your journey, and the good that will be remembered long after you are gone.

The excitement in sports and the victories in business that we witness are small achievements that give us temporary pleasure (remember the reaction of the business group after having their best quarter ever?). The big win is developing a mindset that will serve you well for the rest of your life, developing your potential to its maximum, understanding how your greatest human achievement stands against all of humanity (getting and maintaining perspective). These are the big wins that you achieve through your experience in life and its subsets: business and sports.

Paradoxical summary

The big picture is part of the paradox of life. While you are focusing on your specialty and your little piece of the world, there is a big picture going on as well. What we believe is "big stuff" can be "small stuff." And the small stuff all adds up to be big stuff. It can be confusing, confounding, and seem downright absurd at times. However, there is a winning mindset for every circumstance. Your challenge is to find it, be it, and move forward.

So what?
- What big wins are you playing for today?
- What small stuff may be big stuff?
- What big stuff may be small stuff?

The End of the Beginning

ARE YOU AT the end of your rope? End of your day? End of your patience? End of your training? Wherever you are, it is at the end of something and the beginning of something else. The miraculous thing is that you get to design what that beginning is.

What I like to remind people is that you cannot change anyone else. You can change yourself and you can start right now. The choice is yours. Are you ready to develop the mindset needed to be successful? These chapters are only a guideline. Don't let the ideas in this book be handcuffs. They are meant to be handrails.

Go. Start a new beginning. Develop a game winning mindset. As my friend Gary Mack said, "The greatest victory is the victory over ourselves."

FOR MORE INFORMATION, please feel free to email me at dalimena@creativquest.com or check out our web site at www.CreativQuest.com for a free download of the Field Guide (the journal) for The Winning Mindset for Leadership.

All the Best in Your Successful Quest,
Vision your view
Of a successful You
And let a Higher Power take care of the Rest.

Bibliography

Amen, Dr. Daniel G. *Change Your Brain Change Your Life*. New York: Three Rivers Press, 1998.

Bennis, Warren and Deborah Stevens. *Douglas McGregor Revisited*. Hoboken: John Wiley and Sons, 2008. This book highlights the continuing relevance of McGregor's work from the '60s when he argued for a more humane workplace.

Berra, Yogi. *The Yogi Book*. New York: Workman, 1998.

Bolles, Richard. *What Color is Your Parachute?* Berkeley: Ten Speed Press, 2008. Considered the Bible of job search processes.

Buckingham, Marcus and Curt Coffman. *First, Break All the Rules*. New York: Simon and Schuster, 1999. I like the research and huge sampling size of this work.

Byme, Rhonda. *The Secret*. New York: Atria, 2006. This is a great synthesis of research about successful people who use their minds to create their realities.

Castaneda, Carlos. *Journey to Ixtlan*. New York: Pocket, 1974. Casteneda wrote extensively about his mythical figure, Don Juan, a Yaqui wise man. A "cubic centimeter of opportunity" was in reference to many forces coming together to create what many have come to call a "window of opportunity."

Chopra, Deepak. *The Seven Spiritual Laws of Success*. Novato: Amber Allen Publishing and New World Library, 1994. The author takes you through a series of laws that relate to the unseen (the unmanifest as he states) that result in the seen (the manifest). Mindset is unseen. However, it can be felt. Chopra offers great insight into this unseen but felt journey.

Collins, Jim. *Good to Great*. New York: HarperCollins Publishers, 2001. This is one of the great business books of the last two decades.

Csikszentmihalyi, Mihaly. *Flow: The Psychology of Optimal Experience.* New York: Harper Perennial, 1990.

Daniels, Aubrey. *Bringing Out the Best in People.* New York: McGraw-Hill, 1999. Daniels challenges what most business people do to encourage and motivate the workforce.

Farson, Richard. *Management of the Absurd.* New York: Simon and Schuster, 1996. One of my favorites for focusing on the confounding element of human interaction and participation in organizational life.

Fiorina, Carly. Tough Choices, New York: Penguin Books, 2006.

Gladwell, Malcolm. *Blink: The Power of Thinking Without Thinking.* New York: Little Brown and Company, 2005.

Godin, Seth. *The Dip.* New York: Penguin Group, 2007. Interesting little book that challenges the notion of "winners never quit."

Goleman, Daniel. *Emotional Intelligence.* New York: Bantam Books, 1995.

Goleman, Daniel. *Social Intelligence.* New York: Bantam Books, 2006. Goleman is a science writer and does a great job of making the science readable.

Hawkins, Dr. David. *Power Versus Force: The Hidden Determinants of Human Behavior.* Carlsbad: Hay House, 2002. This is one of those books that I found hard to get through and mind-blowing at the same time.

Kotter, John and Holer Rathgeber. *Our Iceberg Is Melting.* New York: St. Martin's Press, 2005.

Kuhn, Thomas. *The Scientific Structure of Revolution.* Chicago: University of Chicago Press, 1970. Considered the classic book on change. It is a good read for anyone trying to comprehend change dynamics.

Lin, Sing. "Optimum Strategies for Creativity and Longevity." March 2002 paper. This research should concern all people in organizations. This article has much coverage on web sites. A conflicting research report was done in 2005. More research is needed.

Loehr, Jim and Tony Schwartz. *The Power of Full Engagement.* New York: Simon and Schuster, 2003. The authors argue for energy management being more important than time management in business.

Machiavelli, Niccolo. *The Prince.* New York: Knopf, 1908. Considered the classic study on leadership. Although seen as manipulative and pejorative today, Machiavelli was just applying for a job during a difficult time in human history.

Mack, Gary and David Casstevens. *Mind Gym.* New York: Contemporary Books, 2001. This book is written by my friend and sports psychologist Gary Mack and sports writer David Casstevens. I refer to his work and reflection often as his quest for the correct mindset in sports personalities was identical to my own work with business leaders.

Miller, Richard. *Personal Accountability.* Brighton: Denver Press, 1998. Miller does an excellent job of bringing this concept to life by way of learning to ask the "question behind the question."

Pink, Daniel. *Free Agent Nation.* New York: Warner Business Books, 2001.

Restak, Dr. Richard. *The New Brain.* Emmaus: Rodale Press, Emmaus, 2003. Good reference about how we might be influencing the development of the twenty-first century brain.

Ruiz, Don Miguel. *The Four Agreements.* San Raphael: Amber-Allen Publishing, 1997.

Russell, Bill. *Russell Rules: 11 Lessons on Leadership.* New York: Penguin, 2001.

Senge, Peter, C. Otto Scharmer, Joseph Jarworski, Betty Sue Flowers. *Presence: An Exploration of Profound Change in People, Organizations, and Society.* New York, Currency Books, Random House, 2005. Rigorous critical thinking applied to human potential is the best way to describe this book written by people deep into understanding and influence in that very movement.

Senn, Larry and John Childress. *Secret of a Winning Culture.* New York: The Leadership Press, 1999.

Tolle, Eckhart. *A New Earth.* New York: Penguin Books, 2005.

Weider, Marcia. *Life Is But a Dream.* New York: MasterMedia Limited, 1996.

Welch, Jack. *The Four Es of Leadership.* New York: McGraw-Hill, 2005.

Welch, Jack. *Jack: Straight from the Gut.* New York: Warner Books, 2001.

Whyte, William H., Jr. *The Organization Man.* New York: Simon and Schuster, 1956. Fascinating exploration of organizational life as it was evolving in the '50s. Although used in a pejorative sense, all organizations need some sense of marching forward together or else anarchy may result. The saying "too many chiefs and not enough Indians" comes to mind.

Ziglar, Zig. *Top Performance.* Grand Rapids: Baker Publishing, 2003.

Footnotes

[1] Tolle, *A New Earth*.

[2] Yogi Berra was a Hall of Fame baseball player with the New York Yankees from 1946–1963, and then managed the New York Mets and New York Yankees to World Championships.

[3] For more information on systemic thinking, see the work of Ludwig von Bertalanffy or recent books like *Systems Thinking: Managing Chaos and Complexity* by Jamshid Gharajedaghi.

[4] www.WorldViewEyes.com

[5] Mack, *Mind Gym*.

[6] Russell, *Russell Rules: 11 Lessons on Leadership*.

[7] FirstTeam refers to thinking about this team as your first team; in the case of senior leadership, this means looking at the senior team as your first team versus your finance team or HR team, etc.

[8] Senge, *Presence, An Exploration of Profound Change in People, Organizations, and Society*.

[9] Jennings and Haughton, *It's Not the Big That Eat the Small… It's the Fast That Eat the Slow; How to Use Speed as a Competitive Tool in Business*

[10] Castenada, *Journey to Ixtlan*.

[11] Mack, *Mind Gym*.

[12] See *BusinessWeek*, October 2007.

[13] In an eponymous mood one day and after reading *Freakonomics*, I decided the force field of human behavior and economics needed a name. This is the study of the change in human behavior where money is involved, money being one of the many forces of motivation and/or exchange.

[14] Mack, *Mind Gym*.

[15] Selye, *The Stress of Life*.

[16] Eifrig, S&A Health Report.

[17] A dissipative system is characterized by the spontaneous appearance of symmetry breaking (anisotropy) and the formation of complex, sometimes chaotic structures, where interacting particles exhibit long range correlations. The term *dissipative structure* was coined by Prigogine.

[18] Amen, *Change Your Brain Change Your Life*.

[19] Ruiz, *The Four Agreements*.

[20] Mack, *Mind Gym*.

21 Collins, *Good to Great*.
22 Mack, *Mind Gym*.
23 Miller, *Personal Accountability*.
24 Mack, *Mind Gym*.
25 Buckingham, *First, Break All the Rules*..
26 Mack, *Mind Gym*.
27 Bolles, *What Color is Your Parachute?*
28 Kuhn, *The Scientific Structure of Revolution*.
29 Machiavelli, *The Prince*.
30 Lin, "Optimum Strategies for Creativity and Longevity."
31 Ibid.
32 Mack, *Mind Gym*.
33 Chopra, *The Seven Spiritual Laws of Success*.
34 Bennis, *Douglas McGregor Revisited*.
35 Loehr, *The Power of Full Engagement*.
36 Collins, *Good to Great*.
37 Godin, *The Dip*.
38 Collins, *Good to Great*.
39 Mack, *Mind Gym*.
40 Collins, *Good to Great*.
41 Pink, *Free Agent Nation*.
42 Mack, *Mind Gym*.
43 Buckingham, *First, Break All The Rules*.
44 Daniels, *Bringing Out the Best in People*.
45 Hawkins, *Power Versus Force: The Hidden Determinants of Human Behavior*.
46 Wikipedia reference
47 Senn, *Secret of a Winning Culture*.
48 Welch, *The Four Es of Leadership*.
49 Mack, *Mind Gym*., 127.
50 Restak, *The New Brain*.
51 Mack, *Mind Gym*.
52 Ibid. 147.
53 Berra, *The Yogi Book*.
54 Ziglar, *Top Performance*.
55 Mack, *Mind Gym*.
56 Goleman, *Emotional Intelligence*.
57 Goleman, Daniel. *Social Intelligence*.

[58] Mack, *Mind Gym*. 170.
[59] Csikszentmihalyi, *Flow*.
[60] Pink, *Free Agent Nation*.
[61] Farson, *Management of the Absurd*.
[62] Chopra, *The Seven Spiritual Laws of Success*.
[63] Gladwell, *Blink*.
[64] Mack, *Mind Gym*.
[65] Collins, *Good to Great*.
[66] Mack, Mind Gym. (as reported in and the text is my own recollection of data that connects to the Harvard Ls.)

Printed in the United States
209745BV00001B/354/P